Praise for *The Ethics of Protection*

"Through illuminating case studies, impressive theological insights and deep social analysis, this volume explores critical issues in this nation's child protection system. Consistently mindful of endemic structural racism and related systemic injustices, the author probes the boundaries between the conventionally adversarial claims of parental rights and the best interests of vulnerable children. The reader comes away with bold new perspectives on social policy, racial justice, and human moral agency itself—all informed by a liberationist perspective that generates valuable counter-narratives capable of challenging oppressive practices."

—Thomas Massaro, SJ, professor of moral theology, Fordham University, and author of *United States Welfare Policy: A Catholic Response*

"Western epistemology since the 1600s has had difficulty in addressing nature and social challenges with a holistic perspective. The Cartesian method of dividing to understand and control is the dominant way to approach not only the investigation of the natural sciences, but also societal structures and ethical challenges. This is visible in CPS and its way of looking at a child's maltreatment and parental neglect of care. It focuses on the most visible fragment of the problem, dismissing the entirety of the societal issue, that includes structures of violence, history of systemic racism, and the reality of families who are failing to care for their children. Rice's book does not fall into this limitation.

"From a liberating ethical perspective that includes narratives of families who have lost their children, as well as historical and sociological analyses of racism and oppressive structures, Rice offers a comprehensive account on child welfare in the US. *The Ethics of Protection* shows that a society cannot protect its vulnerable children if it does not look at families and the oppressive reality they experience. The author invites us to be sensitive to the stories of these families and attentive

to the violent structures that make these families, and thus their children, suffer. Separating them does not address the problem, but only remediates a visible fragment, contributing to the maintenance of the existing violent structure."

—Alexandre A. Martins, associate professor, Marquette University, and author of *The Cry of the Poor: Liberation Ethics and Justice in Health Care*

"Lincoln Rice gives a voice to families whose own voices are ignored due to their being poor and lacking resources, and who are persecuted in the court system. As Rice documents, CPS does not afford any funding to help individuals attain safety or stability to preserve the sanctity of family. Instead, it actually demolishes the family unit by means of federal adoption subsidies and legislative time limits that force adoption."

—Amada Morales, family advocate

"We applaud the author's conclusion that to attack the racist, classist, and sexist Child Protection Services that separates families and harms children, money must be wrested from the massive child welfare and anti-poverty industries and instead be used to provide proper support to impoverished families. We know that when welfare was cut to undermine Black single mothers, money for the child removal industry increased by 20,000 percent—from $25 million to $5 billion! To remove children unjustly from their mothers dismisses the bond between mother and child and causes long-lasting harm, as the grassroots women who contributed so much to the book describe. Raising children is work, and those doing it are workers. The author calls for a guaranteed income; we are calling for a guaranteed care income. This would change the narrative of the 'undeserving poor,' tackle the poverty of mothers and children (73 percent of the poor), and undermine the practice of removing children from their homes because poverty is considered neglect. Thank you for moving this agenda forward!"

—Margaret Prescod and Phoebe Jones,
Give Us Back Our Children

THE ETHICS OF PROTECTION

THE ETHICS OF PROTECTION

REIMAGINING CHILD WELFARE IN AN ANTI-BLACK SOCIETY

LINCOLN RICE

FORTRESS PRESS
Minneapolis

THE ETHICS OF PROTECTION
Reimagining Child Welfare in an Anti-Black Society

Library of Congress Cataloging-in-Publication Data

Names: Rice, Lincoln, author.
Title: The ethics of protection : reimagining child welfare in an anti-Black society / Lincoln Rice.
Description: Minneapolis : Fortress Press, [2023] | Includes bibliographical references and index.
Identifiers: LCCN 2023008335 | ISBN 9781506494067 (paperback) | ISBN 9781506494074 (ebook)
Subjects: LCSH: Child welfare—United States. | Racism—United States. | White people—United States. | African American families.
Classification: LCC HV741 .R53 2023 | DDC 362.70973—dc23/eng/20230513
LC record available at https://lccn.loc.gov/2023008335

Cover image: Double Dutch illustration by Kristin Miller
Cover design: Angela Griner

Print ISBN: 978-1-5064-9406-7
eBook ISBN: 978-1-5064-9407-4

Contents

Acknowledgments

I would like to acknowledge my debt to the Catholic Worker movement. My time with the Casa Maria Catholic Worker in Milwaukee has brought me into contact with scores of amazing people, including my wife, Laura Pope. I would also like to thank Ryan Hemmer at Fortress Press. He was immediately supportive of this project and provided wonderful feedback.

Most of all, I would like to thank Amada Morales. You will read about Amada in these pages. She is another person I met because of my involvement with Casa Maria. Amada has dedicated herself to being a resource for parents with Child Protective Services cases. Without Amada, I would have remained ignorant of this issue and the resistance stories that you will find in these pages. It has been my privilege to know Amada and work with her. Without her generosity in sharing so much of her experience with me, this book could not have happened.

Therefore, I dedicate this book to Amada Morales and her children, Jordan, Max, and Amado.

Introduction

The intersection of Child Protective Services (CPS) and anti-Black racism in the United States came to my attention because of my involvement with the Casa Maria Catholic Worker and the Welfare Warriors. Both organizations are located in Milwaukee, Wisconsin, and provide support for mothers having their children removed by CPS. Casa Maria is an intentional community that offers temporary housing for homeless families. It differs from the typical shelter in that the community members are not paid, live on the premises, and invite homeless families to stay with them in their home. The Welfare Warriors "are mothers and children in poverty who have joined together to make [their] voices heard in all policies affecting families in poverty."[1] Both Casa Maria and Welfare Warriors have committed time and resources to support parents whose lives have been disrupted by CPS. This includes support meetings, court support, information for parents regarding their legal rights, temporary housing, protests to raise awareness of an issue, and continued dialogue with CPS staff as well as judges, lawyers, and state lawmakers. While I have collaborated with Welfare Warriors sporadically over the years, I have been a continual member of the Casa Maria community since 1998.

My first detailed interaction with CPS occurred when a mother staying at Casa Maria had her young triplets removed. (To protect her identity and the identities of other families in this book, I will use pseudonyms and change some of

1 Welfare Warriors, "Our Mission," n.d., http://www.welfarewarriors.org/mission.htm (accessed March 3, 2019).

the insignificant details.) Angel was a thirty-three-year-old African American with a fifteen-year-old daughter and triplets who were three months old. Angel was staying at Casa Maria because she had lost her job during her pregnancy and became homeless. She had applied for and was receiving welfare, but the maximum monthly welfare payment in the State of Wisconsin is $653. This small amount was not enough to pay her rent and other expenses. Her teenager was a wonderful child who was extremely polite and helpful. While Angel was staying with us, her triplets began vomiting their formula. After a couple days, she was desperate and tried feeding them solid food, but they kept vomiting anything she tried to feed them. On the fourth day, she brought them to their pediatrician. The doctor diagnosed the triplets as having the flu and began treatment. The triplets fully recovered without any further issue.

Angel had been transparent with the physician and confessed that in her desperation, she had tried giving solid food to the triplets. The doctor pointed out that the triplets were too young for solid food, which is something Angel already knew. Though he believed her intentions were good, the physician felt obligated to report the incident to CPS. Shortly afterward, a CPS investigator determined that the triplets were in imminent danger and placed them in foster care. It would be eighteen months until the children were returned to their mother's custody.

As a white Catholic theologian, I am aware that racism was usually ignored—and often reinforced—by white Catholic theologians in the past. Because of the scarcity of anti-racist sources in the Catholic tradition, I will supplement my own theological tradition with the insights and wisdom of Black Protestant theologians and scholars. I would like to echo the sentiment of the white Catholic theologian Katie Grimes, who stated the following in her book *Fugitive Saints*: "I can never stand outside of my whiteness; I ought never be the final judge of my attempts to oppose white-supremacist forms of embodiment."[2] Though I have written this book in careful collaboration with activists of color struggling against the CPS apparatus, the findings herein are tentative until confirmed and augmented by the experience of Black families in the United States.

PURPOSE OF THIS BOOK

This book is a theology book, but it will also be useful for students and others interested in the ethics of social work. This task will be accomplished by employing a liberationist perspective for social welfare ethics. A liberationist perspective is distinctive from traditional Christian ethics in two key ways: (1) its critique of neoliberal politics and economics and (2) the movement of the social location of ethics from governing bodies, boardrooms, and institutions to the perspective of those most vulnerable in society.[3]

Regarding the first point, neoliberal politics promote a free market economy, privatization of natural resources and government programs, and deregulation. In addition, a free market economy affects the number and quality of resources at one's disposal. As a result of neoliberal policies in the United States, one's freedom is affected by the amount of money at one's disposal; one's access to quality housing, education, and medical care; one's sex, gender, and the color of one's skin.

CPS and social work do not occur in a vacuum but in a society with a culture and mechanisms for enforcing

2 Katie Walker Grimes, *Fugitive Saints: Catholicism and the Politics of Slavery* (Minneapolis: Fortress Press, 2017), 56.

3 M. Therese Lysaught and Michael McCarthy, "A Social Praxis for US Health Care: Revisioning Catholic Bioethics via Catholic Social Thought," *Journal of the Society of Christian Ethics* 38, no. 2 (fall/winter 2018): 111–30, on p. 121.

a culture's values. The freedom of social workers and social work students who are reading this book will be restricted by the culture and mechanisms present in their schools and workplaces. In most workplaces, social workers need to act respectfully toward their managers regardless of whether this respect is reciprocated. Disrespecting one's manager in person or on social media can lead to unemployment. US society likes to portray itself as one in which the individual has complete freedom, but complete freedom is not possible in any society. More will be said on freedom later.

Regarding the second point on social location, this book is inspired by the perspective of those most affected by CPS: the parents and children who, too often, are separated without any proven instance of maltreatment. Without having had come into contact with these courageous mothers, I would have lacked the proper perspective to write this book. It is crucial to realize that the perspective of Black mothers in this scenario is not simply one of vulnerability and poverty. These mothers are brave, creative, and inspirational. Their actions are a juncture point for societal transformation and life-giving activity.[4] Therefore, my hope is that the material and stories found in this book will also be a resource for families who have been accosted by CPS, as well as lawmakers, judges, lawyers, foster parents, social workers, social work students, and anyone else involved with some aspect of CPS. Although this book is not a guide for how social workers can act ethically in their position of power, it has broad implications for social workers and anyone else involved with the CPS apparatus.

4 This last point about communities that are "marginalized and vulnerable" also being "transformative and generative" is superbly highlighted in Janna L. Hunter-Bowman, "Constructive Agents under Duress: Alternatives to the Structural, Political, and Agential Inadequacies of Past Theologies of Nonviolent Peacebuilding Efforts," *Journal of the Society of Christian Ethics* 38, no. 2 (fall/winter 2018): 149–68, on pp. 149–50.

This book fills a gap in the literature regarding ethics for CPS. There are countless books and articles on the topic of CPS policy, but little is available that scrutinizes CPS from an ethical standpoint. This is even more so when the issue of anti-Black racism is involved. The only book with a strong critique of the anti-Black racism inherent in CPS is Dorothy Roberts's recent *Torn Apart: How the Child Welfare System Destroys Black Families—And How Abolition Can Build a Safer World*.[5] Roberts's book exposes the current configuration of CPS as a form of "family policing" that has its roots in US slavery and the Black Codes to restrict the freedom of African Americans. Although our books have many things in common, this book examines more closely the history and daily workings of CPS. Additionally, Roberts is confronting this topic from a sociological perspective, whereas this book addresses the topic from the standpoint of theological ethics.

There is also *Child Abuse, Family Rights, and the Child Protective System: A Critical Analysis from Law, Ethics, and Catholic Social Teaching* (2013),[6] but this is a presentation of conference papers that are uneven in quality and essentially ignores the issue of race. There is also *Working Ethically in Child Protection* (2016) by Bob Lonne, Maria Harries, Brid Featherstone, and Mel Gray,[7] whose primary audience is CPS social workers in Australia and the United Kingdom. Their book employs a values- and principles-based model to critique CPS, which is supposed to observe all aspects of the problem and consider various options—all in light of the

5 Dorothy Roberts, *Torn Apart: How the Child Welfare System Destroys Black Families—And How Abolition Can Build a Safer World* (New York: Basic Books, 2022).

6 Stephen M. Krason, ed., *Child Abuse, Family Rights, and the Child Protective System: A Critical Analysis from Law, Ethics, and Catholic Social Teaching* (Lanham, MD: Scarecrow Press, 2013).

7 Bob Lonne et al., *Working Ethically in Child Protection* (New York: Routledge, 2016).

principles of care, respect, and justice—before deciding on an ethical course of action. This is an important and helpful book for social workers, but it does not significantly address anti-Black racism in the United States.[8] It should be noted that values- and principles-based models have traditionally been a European manner of examining problems. The weakness in this model is that it often mistakes its principles as an unbiased starting point, which does not actually exist. Not surprisingly, principles-based models often neglect the issue of racism.

In contrast, a liberationist perspective believes the formation of ethical responses begins with the experience of the oppressed. It is only in this way that the experiences and insights gained from the perspective of the oppressed will not be omitted, ignored, or forgotten. The liberationist perspective found in this book begins in the troubling experiences of families—particularly African American families—caught in the CPS apparatus. Those experiences are the foundational perspective from which the entire CPS system in the United States must be evaluated.

In 1979, the African American novelist James Baldwin wrote "Open Letter to the Born Again," in which he proclaimed, "I am in the strenuous and far from dull position of having news to deliver to the Western world—for example: *Black* is not a synonym for *slave.* Do not, I counsel you, attempt to defend yourselves against this stunning, unwieldly and undesired message. You will hear it again: indeed, this is the only message the Western world is likely to be hearing from here on out."[9]

This was Baldwin's message to Christians in the Western world over forty years ago, and it will be a regular theme in

8 Lonne et al., *Working Ethically in Child Protection*, 156–62.

9 James Baldwin, "Open Letter to the Born Again," in *James Baldwin: Collected Essays*, ed. Toni Morrison (New York: Library of America, 1998), 784. Emphasis in the original.

this book. This book aims to break open the warning that James Baldwin gave in a post-slavery, post–Jim Crow United States and illustrate its continued relevance in the twenty-first century. Only after the acknowledgment that *Black* and *slave* are treated as synonyms in American society can we work toward creating a world where that is no longer the case. This reality has also been called the *afterlife of slavery*. This term was coined by Saidiya Hartman as a way of expressing the lasting connection and influence that Black slavery continues to have on US life and culture.[10] For example, African American children during the time of slavery were under the legal control of white families and could be killed by their "owners" or sold to another family. Today, Black children can be killed in the streets by police officers or removed from their parents by CPS—often without any legal redress.

DEFINITIONS CONCERNING RACE

The Black liberation theologian Bryan Massingale has noted that *race* is a "troublesome term."[11] *Race* has "limited *scientific* usefulness" and speaks more to a cultural, social, and political reality.[12] As Ibram X. Kendi notes, since the mapping of the entire human genome in 2000, scientists cannot determine a person's race from their genetic code. In fact, they note greater differences in the genetic code of individuals of the same race than between individuals of different races.[13]

Therefore, I want to be clear about how terms regarding race should be understood in this book by defining six terms:

10 Saidiya Hartman, *Lose Your Mother: A Journey along the Atlantic Slave Route* (New York: Farrar, Straus, and Giroux, 2008), 6.

11 Bryan N. Massingale, *Racial Justice and the Catholic Church* (Maryknoll, NY: Orbis Books, 2010), 3.

12 Massingale, *Racial Justice*, 3. Italics in the original.

13 Ibram X. Kendi, *Stamped from the Beginning* (New York: Nation Books, 2016), 474–76.

race, *racism*, *anti-Black racism*, *anti-racism*, *racial liberalism*, and *racial indifference*. I will employ the following definition of *racism*: "Racism is a cultural phenomenon that creates institutionalized patterns of discrimination against people of color so as to consolidate and bestow power and privilege to white people."[14] According to this definition, white people benefit from racism whether or not they acknowledge it. In addition, racism can be, and often is, inadvertently perpetuated.

Anti-Black racism is a term that focuses specifically on racism that harms African Americans. When racism is mentioned in this book, it will primarily be referring to the racism experienced by African Americans. The history, stereotypes, and discrimination faced by each nonwhite group in the United States are unique, and each group's interaction with CPS has its own unique history.

Furthermore, any work on the interactions between Latinx/Hispanic families and CPS will face substantial challenges since Hispanics may identify as Hispanic, white, Black, or Native American depending on their situation, which makes it more difficult to produce accurate statistics. The racial group most disproportionately affected by CPS is Native American. The trials they have endured with CPS as well as their mistreatment for centuries in North America by the US government are significant. Although in the State of Wisconsin, CPS agencies report substantiated cases of maltreatment against African American children at a proportion that is over twice as high as their population, Native American children are reported at a rate of nearly three times their population.[15] As this book's focus is dedicated to the

14 Midwest Catholic Worker Faith and Resistance Gathering 2017, "Lament. Repent. Repair.: An Open Letter on Racism to the Catholic Worker Movement," *Catholic Worker Anti-Racism Review*, spring 2018, 2–4, on p. 2.

15 Wisconsin Department of Children and Families, *Wisconsin Child Abuse and Neglect Report: Annual Report for Calendar Year 2019*, par. 4.5. African American children are 11.1 percent of the Wisconsin

plight of African American families, space considerations do not permit the proper examination of the situation of Native American and Hispanic families.

Anti-racism refers to intentional acts to create a culture in which institutionalized patterns of discrimination against people of color are deemed unacceptable and are rectified. An anti-racist attributes the problems faced by Black people to a racist system. This is the reason anti-racists work to correct institutional and structural forms of racism.[16] This last point may be further clarified by defining *racial liberalism*, which describes a mindset that does not tolerate "overt bigotry" but leaves institutional or structural forms of racism largely unaddressed. This viewpoint underestimates the "advantages and privileges that have accumulated in the white population because of the past history of discrimination," believing that the elimination of overt discrimination alone is an adequate response to racism without any need for restorative policies.[17]

Another important perspective on anti-Black racism has been recently promoted by Michelle Alexander. She observes that both the Jim Crow laws of the early and mid-twentieth century and the mass incarceration of the late twentieth and early twenty-first centuries relied not so much on racial hatred but "far more on *racial indifference* (defined as a lack of compassion and caring about race and racial groups)."[18]

---

population and are reported victims of maltreatment 25.4 percent of the time. Wisconsin reports for different years can be found at https://dcf.wisconsin.gov/cwportal/reports.

16 Kendi, *Stamped from the Beginning*, 2–4.

17 The definition of *racial liberalism* is adapted from Charles W. Mills, *Black Rights/White Wrongs* (New York: Oxford University Press, 2017), 158–59, 203; and Nils Gilman, "End of an Era: The Collapse of Racial Liberalism," *American Interest* 13, no. 5 (2018), https://www.the-american-interest.com/2018/03/02/collapse-racial-liberalism.

18 Michelle Alexander, *The New Jim Crow*, rev. ed. (New York: The New Press, 2012), 203. Emphasis in the original.

Even during slavery, the majority of white plantation owners did not actively hate Blacks but chose to take advantage of slavery to become rich. Or, as Alexander states, they were "indifferent to the suffering caused by slavery, they were motivated by greed."[19] Similarly, I will argue that it is the attitude of racial indifference by white Americans combined with a belief in racial liberalism that permitted the creation and perpetuation of an anti-Black CPS culture.

Anti-Black racism alone does not account for this suppression of freedom; poverty and sexism are also important. We see here the reality of intersectionality, in which we encounter the "complexities of compoundedness" in the realm of oppression.[20] Racism, classism, and sexism each have unique attributes, but they can also reinforce one another and form unique oppressions. For example, the discrimination faced by an impoverished Black woman will have the unique quality of racism, classism, and sexism, but the combination of these -isms will also create forms of discrimination unique to impoverished Black women. There will be challenges faced by impoverished Black women that are not faced by white women, unemployed white men, or Black men. And someone cannot simply combine the oppressions faced by white women (sexism), unemployed white men (classism), and Black men (racism) to discern how racism, classism, and sexism will affect an impoverished Black woman.

So what is the point of this discussion on intersectionality? The fruitful result of this analysis is the insight that the oppression faced by an impoverished Black woman will not be solved by addressing racism, classism, and sexism

19 Alexander, *New Jim Crow*, 203–4.

20 The expression "complexities of compoundedness" is from Kimberle Crenshaw, "Demarginalizing the Intersection of Race and Sex: A Black Feminist Critique of Antidiscrimination Doctrine, Feminist Theory and Antiracist Politics," *University of Chicago Legal Forum* (1989): 139–67, on p. 166.

separately. Working on these issues individually may improve the lives of white women, unemployed white men, and Black men, but it would not likely improve the lives of impoverished Black women. It is also important to address intersectionality because the lives of impoverished Black women and their children are disproportionately facing oppression in the current CPS system.

SOME BASIC INFORMATION ON CPS

In 2020, there were 73 million children in the United States and approximately 618,000 substantiated victims of child neglect and abuse. This equals roughly 8.4 victims of child maltreatment for every 1,000 children. In 2020, about 217,000 children entered foster care, meaning that 3.0 children out of every 1,000 were placed in foster care.[21] African American children are almost twice as likely to be deemed victims of child abuse as white children. Per 1,000 children, 13.2 African American children are judged to be victims of child maltreatment compared to 7.4 white children.[22] Regarding out-of-home care, Black children are three times as likely to be removed from the home compared to white children and represent 23 percent of children currently in out-of-home placement.[23]

21 Children's Bureau of the US, *Child Maltreatment 2020,* ii, xi, https://www.acf.hhs.gov/cb/report/child-maltreatment-2020 (accessed March 26, 2023); Children's Bureau of the US, "Trends in Foster Care and Adoption: FY 2012–2021," 1, https://www.acf.hhs.gov/sites/default/files/documents/cb/trends-foster-care-adoption-2012-2021.pdf.

22 Statista Research Department, "Child Abuse Rate in the U.S.—Victims 2020, by Race/Ethnicity," January 26, 2022, https://www.statista.com/statistics/254857/child-abuse-rate-in-the-us-by-race-ethnicity/ (accessed February 25, 2022).

23 Children's Bureau, *The AFCARS Report,* no. 25, November 8, 2018, 2, https://www.acf.hhs.gov/cb/report/afcars-report-25 (accessed March

The COVID-19 pandemic has affected some of these statistics, but the disproportionality between Black and white families in regard to their interactions with CPS has remained largely unchanged. After schools had closed during the early days of the pandemic, there was great concern among CPS advocates that child maltreatment would skyrocket with children being at home and out of sight of mandatory reporters like teachers.[24] During a neighborhood Zoom meeting I attended at the time, local police shared this same concern and asked attendees to report any suspected instance of child maltreatment.

A statistic that is easier to track even during a pandemic is child deaths that are determined to be caused by maltreatment. In 2019—the year before the pandemic—there were 1,830 reported child deaths due to maltreatment. In 2020—the first year of the pandemic—the number dropped to 1,750.[25] It is telling that the number of child deaths dropped in the same year that CPS interacted with far fewer families because teachers and doctors were not able to report

3, 2023). For 2020, Black children were 1.6 times more likely to be removed from the home compared to white children. The exact reason for this drop is unknown, but likely it is COVID-19 related. Perhaps CPS agencies in urban centers with larger Black populations faced a greater slowdown because of COVID-19 restrictions compared to rural areas. Children's Bureau, *The AFCARS Report,* no. 28, October 4, 2021, 2, https://www.acf.hhs.gov/cb/report/afcars-report-28 (accessed February 26, 2022).

24 Gina Barton, "'No One Is There to Point It Out': Experts Say More Child Abuse Is Likely Happening—but with Kids at Home, It's Not Being Reported," *Milwaukee Journal Sentinel,* May 7, 2020, https://www.jsonline.com/story/news/2020/05/07/wisconsin-child-abuse-reports-plunged-coronavirus-closed-schools/5177780002/ (accessed August 9, 2022).

25 Administration for Children and Families, "Child Fatalities Due to Abuse and Neglect Decreased in FY 2020, Report Finds," January 21, 2022, https://www.acf.hhs.gov/media/press/2022/child-fatalities-due-abuse-and-neglect-decreased-fy-2020-report-finds (accessed August 9, 2022).

suspected maltreatment with children staying at home. If CPS intrusion into homes and the separation of families are supposed to save children's lives, one would assume child deaths would have substantially increased in 2020.

Under federal law, child maltreatment is defined as "any recent act or failure to act on the part of a parent or caretaker which results in death, serious physical or emotional harm, sexual abuse or exploitation" or "an act or failure to act which presents an imminent risk of serious harm."[26] *Child maltreatment* is a blanket term that includes instances of both neglect and abuse. The most common type of maltreatment is child neglect, which accounts for 77.5 percent of reported victims; 15.4 percent of reported victims were physically abused, and 9.6 percent were sexually abused.[27] The definition of child maltreatment above is only meant to be used as a guide by states, which are permitted to create their own definitions of maltreatment.

The State of Wisconsin defines child neglect as the "failure, refusal or inability on the part of a caregiver, for reasons other than poverty, to provide necessary care, food, clothing, medical or dental care or shelter so as to seriously endanger the physical health of the child." It defines physical abuse as "physical injury inflicted on a child by other than accidental means. . . . Physical injury includes but is not limited to lacerations, fractured bones, burns, internal injuries, severe or frequent bruising or great bodily harm."[28] The definition

26 Children's Bureau of the US, *Child Maltreatment 2021,* ix, https://www.acf.hhs.gov/cb/report/child-maltreatment-2021 (accessed March 4, 2023).

27 Children's Bureau of the US, *Child Maltreatment 2021,* 104.

28 Wisconsin Department of Children and Families, *Wisconsin Child Abuse and Neglect Report: Annual Report for Calendar Year 2018 to the Governor and Legislature,* released December 2019, 1.2–1.3, https://dcf.wisconsin.gov/files/cwportal/reports/pdf/can.pdf (accessed March 13, 2020). After this footnote, the report will be referred to as *Wisconsin Report 2018.*"

of sexual abuse is very detailed, and it is complicated by the several degrees of sexual abuse. Thankfully, it is the least common form of child abuse. Because of the complexity of the definition, the rarity of occurrence in CPS cases, and this type of abuse not being the focus of this book, a definition will not be provided here.

The national data for maltreatment should not be considered the actual numbers of child-maltreatment cases in the United States. This data is based on determinations made by CPS workers all over the country. Some believe these numbers represent a smaller percentage of a larger problem. This book argues that the statistics overstate the problem and that CPS workers often err on the side of making a maltreatment determination, which results in too many children being needlessly removed from their homes. A key factor to recognize at this point is that the most common type of maltreatment is neglect, which indicates a CPS investigator's belief that a parent cannot adequately care for a child. Determining factors, whether conscious or unconscious, often include poverty, race, and cultural factors that make the investigator uncomfortable with permitting the child to stay with a parent.

Unfortunately, news coverage concerning child maltreatment often focuses on the most horrific cases of child abuse. The story is even more compelling if the child's case was already being addressed by CPS, but the child had not been removed. Sometimes, the CPS worker clearly had enough evidence to justify child removal but did not. The actual or perceived failures of CPS workers to remove children in these cases cause public scandal and pressure CPS workers to err on the side of unnecessarily removing children from their parents. Within the CPS literature, this dynamic is termed the *routinization of outrage*.[29]

29 Michael J. Camasso and Radha Jagannathan, "Decision Making in Child Protective Services: A Risky Business?" *Risk Analysis* 33, no. 9 (2013): 1636–49, on pp. 1637, 1644.

FOCUS ON WISCONSIN

You may have already noticed several references to CPS in the State of Wisconsin. Although this book is a general critique of the child welfare system in the United States, it will often provide specific examples from Wisconsin. The primary reason for this is that the situation in Wisconsin is the one I am most familiar with and can speak with the greatest authority on. Part of this is due to my personal experiences with CPS in Wisconsin through my work at Casa Maria. Another part of this is due to the time I have spent examining Wisconsin CPS reports. Every state publishes CPS reports, but there is no consistency in what they choose to report, especially with racial data. Where I have found Wisconsin's reports lacking, I have been able to solicit supplemental information directly from the Wisconsin Department of Children and Families. Without the supplemental data it has provided for me, I would not have been able to present as accurate a description of child welfare in Wisconsin. This being said, I believe readers in other states will find that their situation resonates with the one in Wisconsin.

STUDY OF ETHICS

Ethics is about values and how those values inform our actions in specific situations. The explicit value that currently defines the child welfare system is the "best interests of the child." Normally, the "best interests of the child" principle is used as justification for removing children from biological parents. This book will explore this principle and argue that it is not the best way to determine when US society should choose to intervene in the lives of families. I will also give *prima facie* priority to the Catholic perspective that the family is the basic building block of society and contributes to the common good. In this way, I will argue for the best interests of the family, particularly the Black family. The best interests of the Black family prioritize authentic freedom, which presupposes racial and economic justice.

As we consider and explore these various principles, we will need to ask several questions: How do we weigh the rights of children against the rights of parents? What is the role of government, and how do we prevent the danger of government overreach? Can the cultural, social, and financial support for white suburbanites looking to adopt the children of Black mothers be justified as financial assistance is withheld from Black families? What role do structural sin, anti-Black racism, classism, and a lack of self-agency have in the child welfare system, and how should society respond?

This book will also investigate and attempt to explain the unjust racial discrimination inherent in CPS's targeting of African Americans, even if this is largely unintentional or an example of racial indifference. As will be covered in the following chapters, the problem stems from a combination of (1) a thoroughgoing cultural and systemic racism in American society and the CPS system, (2) federal and local policies and laws—both intentional and unintentional—that work to undermine the integrity of the Black family, and (3) practices at the local level by poorly trained personnel, many of whom also harbor innate anti-Black racial prejudices.

The Trolley Problem

The "trolley problem" thought experiment will be helpful in delineating the ethical issues at stake in the child welfare system. This experiment has you imagine that a runaway trolley is heading down the tracks toward five people who are incapacitated. If nothing is done, the five people will be killed. You can clearly see the problem and are certain of the result. You happen to be standing next to a lever that can switch the trolley to another set of tracks. On the other set of tracks is a single person who is incapacitated. Should you pull the lever to save five people at the expense of killing one person? This experiment raises the question: Is it better to be directly involved with killing one person or indirectly involved in five preventable deaths? It pits logic against emotion as well as utilitarianism against moral imperatives.

This experiment can also be applied to CPS. In 2020, 1,750 children in the United States died as a result of child abuse or neglect. In 2020, CPS agencies investigated or assessed the situations of 3.1 million children. As a result, 618,000 children were deemed victims of maltreatment, and 173,079 children were placed in foster care.[30] Although no one wants children to die because they were not removed from a dangerous parent, to what extent should we disrupt the lives of millions of families to save the lives of a few thousand children? This question is unsettling, but CPS actions trying to save children from death often cause additional harm. To be a parent of one of the millions of children who are questioned by CPS is disorienting and frightening. To be one of the 173,079 children placed in foster care is often traumatizing. The average stay for a child in foster care is twenty-one months.[31] The sociologists Kristin Turney and Christopher Wildeman portray this information as follows: "Each year, nearly 1% of U.S. children spend time in foster care, with 6% of U.S. children placed in foster care at least once between their birth and 18th birthday."[32] The number is even higher for African American children, with 10 percent entering foster care before turning eighteen.[33]

To complicate this issue further, there is no reliable method for discerning how effective the CPS system is in protecting child safety. As the child welfare researcher Alberta J. Ellett comments, the only sure way to measure

30 Children's Bureau of the US, *Child Maltreatment 2020,* ii, 20, 89.

31 Children's Bureau, *The AFCARS Report,* no. 28, 2.

32 Kristin Turney and Christopher Wildeman, "Mental and Physical Health of Children in Foster Care," *Pediatrics* 138, no. 5 (November 2016): 1, https://pediatrics.aappublications.org/content/pediatrics/138/5/e20161118.full.pdf (accessed April 7, 2019).

33 Turney and Wildeman, "Mental and Physical Health," 2.

the effectiveness of CPS would be to "randomize" half of all reports to CPS and provide CPS services to one half, while the other half would act as a control group and not receive CPS services. Then, after six months or some other determined timeframe, investigate the situation of both groups "to compare the number of maltreated and dead children."[34] Obviously, this cannot be ethically done as it would require workers to ignore what they feel are clear cases of child abuse and neglect. But if such a study could be performed, it would provide information not only about how many children CPS protects but how many children are needlessly removed from their families. Under the current CPS system, it is not possible to measure how many children should not have been removed. It is much easier for media outlets to document the cases of children who should have been removed but were not.

The mere placing of children in foster care has ethical ramifications. A recent study found that children placed in foster care had more mental and physical health conditions than children not placed in foster care. For instance, children placed in foster care were about twice as likely to have a learning disability and three times more likely to have attention deficit disorder (ADD) or attention deficit hyperactivity disorder (ADHD). They were also about twice as likely to have asthma and speech problems and three times more likely to have hearing and vision problems. Differences were even more substantial for other mental health conditions. Children placed in foster care were five times as likely to have anxiety, six times more likely to have behavioral problems, and seven times more likely to suffer from depression.[35]

34 Alberta J. Ellett, "Timely and Needed Perspectives on Differential Response in Child Protective Services," *Research on Social Work Practice* 23, no. 5 (2013): 521–24, on p. 522.

35 Turney and Wildeman, "Mental and Physical Health," 5. It should be noted that their research did not include children group homes or institutions (p. 10).

The authors of the study note that although a portion of these statistics can be explained "by characteristics of these children and their households, many of the differences in mental health persisted after adjusting for these child and household characteristics, indicating a direct effect from a foster care placement on mental health."[36] Another study reveals that children in foster care are four times more likely to attempt suicide than children in the general population. And a California study found that 41 percent of children in foster care have contemplated suicide.[37]

Children in foster care are also almost three times more likely to be prescribed psychotropic drugs than children not in foster care. Depending on the state, 14–50 percent of children in foster care are prescribed psychotropic medication.[38] This raises the question of whether children in states with higher uses of psychotropic medication are being overmedicated. It is difficult to believe that the children located in the states with the lowest and highest rates of psychotropic drug use are so different in their need for this medication. The most commonly prescribed psychotropics are atypical antipsychotics for emotional and behavioral concerns, followed by stimulants for ADHD, then by antidepressants for helping children cope with depression.[39] Though antipsychotics were originally meant to treat schizophrenia and bipolar disorder, youths in foster care are nine times more likely to be prescribed these medications for a use not approved by the Food and Drug Administration (FDA). It is also common for these drugs to be prescribed in doses above those approved

36 Turney and Wildeman, "Mental and Physical Health," 5.

37 Roberts, *Torn Apart*, 235.

38 Sheri Pickover and Heather Brown, *Therapeutic Interventions for Families and Children in the Child Welfare System* (New York: Springer Publishing Company, 2016), 103.

39 Pickover and Brown, *Therapeutic Interventions*, 104.

by the FDA. The possible harmful effects of prolonged use of these drugs on children have not been studied.[40]

There are child welfare professionals who claim that the CPS system too heavily favors the parents at the risk of the children. For example, the sociologist Richard Gelles argues for greater reliance on probability models, which he concedes would likely remove more children from the home and terminate more parents' rights. For him, that is the price of safety.[41] This solution is untenable and reminiscent of the film *Minority Report* (2002). Based on the book of the same name, this science-fiction film imagines a future where people are arrested and found guilty of crimes they have not yet committed. It is the psychic ability of three individuals that is used to determine the inevitability of the crime and pass judgment without any crime being done. In the film, this system is eventually brought into question, just as skepticism should be the appropriate response to the notion of removing children based on the possibility of future maltreatment.

Moreover, foster care possesses such a convoluted and dangerous bureaucracy that the National Coalition for Child Protection Reform refers to it as the "foster care industrial complex."[42] Foster care advocates are blindly assuming that the trolley problem does not apply to foster care. The CPS system cannot assume that placing children in foster care is the "better safe than sorry" solution. The CPS system needs to honestly weigh the possible harm of leaving a child with a parent versus the future health problems that will likely manifest from a child being placed in foster care.

40 Pickover and Brown, *Therapeutic Interventions*, 104.

41 Richard J. Gelles, *Out of Harm's Way: Creating an Effective Child Welfare System* (New York: Oxford University Press, 2017), 84–85.

42 One can easily find this term all over its website at nccpr.org.

CONCLUSION

Perhaps the toughest sell that I will be making in this book is asking the reader to sympathize with parents who have been accused of maltreating their own children. There is almost a visceral reaction to side with children against a parent. But this is usually a false dichotomy. I will not be asking you to decide between the parent and the child. In most cases, sympathizing with the parent is in the best interests of the child. Michelle Alexander notes a similar dilemma in asking her readers to sympathize with African Americans convicted of nonviolent drug crimes. As she states, "Many would argue that expending scarce resources on criminal justice reform is a strategic mistake. After all, criminals are the one social group in America that nearly everyone—across political, racial, and class boundaries—feels free to hate."[43]

When the civil rights movement was looking for a face for the bus boycott, the leadership passed over African Americans who had been previously arrested and specifically chose Rosa Parks. Parks had no skeletons in her closet, was lighter-skinned, and was of impeccable character.[44] But in discussing CPS, we will be bringing forth examples of imperfect parents who are trying to raise their children in difficult circumstances with limited resources. So I will also be asking the reader not to make snap judgments. One's gut can be a source for moral knowledge, but its capacity for assessing complex situations is limited. With this in mind, I propose the following layout to explore the CPS system in an anti-Black culture.

Chapter 1 begins with a brief history and the current state of the child welfare system. Chapter 2 analyzes how anti-Black racism has disproportionately affected African

43 Alexander, *New Jim Crow*, 228.
44 Alexander, *New Jim Crow*, 227.

American families in their interactions with CPS. The role of poverty in causing harmful interactions with CPS for both white and Black families is also addressed in the second chapter. Chapter 3 argues that the history and racist practices of CPS toward Black parents explored in the first two chapters have a theological foundation, a view of human worth and divine dignity rooted in anti-Black ideology. In contrast, Catholic Social Teaching (CST) offers a theological vision of parenthood and childhood and their respective forms of dignity as a liberative alternative to the theological anthropology of anti-Blackness. In chapter 4, an analysis of the Black family in its struggle against CPS will enlighten our understanding of the theology of the biblical Holy Family, who was favored by God despite its poverty and the fear the child Jesus instilled in a hegemonic government. The theological dialogue between the Black family battling CPS and the biblical Holy Family can create a new icon capable of producing a fruitful critique of CPS: the Black Holy Family. Chapter 5 will examine the idea of abolishing CPS, or CPS abolition, as well as offer suggestions for improving the child welfare system that are more in line with CST and the icon of the Black Holy Family.

ONE

A Brief History of Child Welfare

The purpose of this chapter is to provide a brief overview of the history of child welfare services in the United States. It is not meant to be an exhaustive history, but it will lay a foundation for understanding how child welfare evolved to its present form. One might think that since this chapter focuses on the *history* of child welfare, it could be skipped, but I would not recommend that course of action. The history covered in this chapter continues right up to the present. This chapter is required reading to genuinely understand the arguments in the rest of the book. After providing a basic history, there is an examination of the complex Child Protective Services (CPS) apparatus for processing allegations, followed by concluding remarks.

COLONIAL AND EARLY UNITED STATES

In the colonial United States, the rights of children were hardly recognized culturally or legally. Nevertheless, orphaned children and the children of the poorest people were often seen as the responsibility of society. Children of the poorest families might be removed by the colonial governments because the parents could not support them or because the parents were viewed as a bad influence. It was commonly assumed that paupers did not value work or could not pass on a work ethic to their children. A similar narrative has been used to devalue Black parents in the United States during the later twentieth and early twenty-first centuries. Additionally, the high mortality rate from childbearing, disease, war, and other hardships resulted in a high orphan population. To put the problem of orphans in context, there were over 750,000 orphans in the United States in 1920, but by 1970, that number had dropped to less than 2,000.[1]

The first orphanage in the United States was founded in New Orleans in 1727 by the Ursuline Sisters, a Catholic religious order. Prior to this, very young orphans or the children of paupers were often sent to almshouses, which were public institutions that cared for destitute children and adults. Most almshouses admitted a combination of children, indigent adults, those suffering from mental illness, and those who were blind or deaf. Additionally, at eight or nine years old, children were often indentured, meaning they were apprenticed to households where they could learn a trade.[2] This practice did raise questions about the motive of the parents to whom children were indentured. Were the children treated with care and respect as if they were the parents' own children, or were they being exploited as cheap labor? With the end of slavery in 1865, opposition to the indenturing of white children increased, and the practice soon ended.[3] By the mid-nineteenth century, views on placing orphans in almshouses also began to change. Numerous exposés on almshouses and the terrible conditions experienced by children moved public opinion to view them as unsuitable for children.[4]

1 Brenda G. McGowan, "Historical Evolution of Child Welfare Services," in *Child Welfare for the 21st Century*, ed. Gerald P. Mallon and Peg McCartt Hess (New York: Columbia University Press, 2005), 10–46, on p. 11; Duncan Lindsey, *The Welfare of Children* (New York: Oxford University Press, 1994), 11–12.

2 McGowan, "Historical Evolution," 12.

3 McGowan, "Historical Evolution," 12.

4 McGowan, "Historical Evolution," 13; Lindsey, *Welfare of Children*, 12–13.

Foster care began with the founding of the Children's Aid Society in New York by Charles Loring Brace in 1853. Within fifty years, these societies had spread to most major cities on the East Coast. Brace believed poor and orphaned children would be better served by placing them with Christian families in the countryside. By 1875, thirty-five thousand children had been relocated from New York City to foster care, often with farming families in the Midwest. As the child welfare reformer David Tobis explains, "The Orphan Trains of the nineteenth century . . . had the explicit function of protecting New York City from delinquent, immigrant Catholic youth."[5]

Obviously, xenophobia played a large role in support given to the actions of the Children's Aid Society. The total number of children who were relocated grew to ninety-two thousand by 1890. A similar group, called the Children's Home Society, began in 1883 in Illinois and also spread rapidly.[6] Orphanages run by public, private, and religious institutions increased substantially during the 1830s. During the late 1860s and until the end of the nineteenth century, many Catholic and Jewish orphanages were founded in response to many of their children being sent to Protestant homes in the Midwest. These institutions wanted to ensure the children of their respective faith communities could be raised in the faith tradition of their parents.[7]

A shift toward recognizing child abuse as we understand it today occurred in 1873, when Etta Wheeler discovered the severe abuse that ten-year-old orphan Mary Ellen Wilson was receiving from her foster parents. When Wheeler first sought

5 David Tobis, *From Pariahs to Partners* (Oxford: Oxford University Press, 2013), xxiv.

6 McGowan, "Historical Evolution," 14; Lindsey, *Welfare of Children*, 13; Catherine E. Rymph, *Raising Government Children: A History of Foster Care and the American Welfare State* (Chapel Hill: University of North Carolina, 2017), 20–23.

7 Tobis, *From Pariahs to Partners*, 5.

to have Wilson removed, various authorities told her that it was not in their power to remove the child. The animal rights activist Henry Bergh aided her in collecting evidence that was eventually used in court to remove the child from the custody of the foster parents, employing an innovative use of habeas corpus and successfully prosecuting the foster mother for assault and battery. The national publicity associated with the court case led to an expanded role for the state in removing children from families for child maltreatment.[8] As cities began passing legislation in the 1870s to "protect" children from cruel parents, the rhetoric to promote such legislation focused on the harm caused by alcoholic immigrant fathers, which eventually was superseded by arguments of protecting children from the neglect of impoverished parents.[9]

BLACK CHILDREN BEFORE AND AFTER THE CIVIL WAR

African American children faced additional difficulties. Before the Civil War, enslaved Black children were legally the property of the slave master, not their parents. The Slave Act of 1807, which outlawed the transatlantic slave trade, complicated matters even more for enslaved Blacks in the United States. There was now more of an emphasis on "breeding" Black captives within the United States to meet the continual demand for slave labor. An 1809 South Carolina court case confirmed that Black captive children "could be sold away from their mothers at any age because the young slaves stand on the same footing as other animals."[10] The

8 McGowan, "Historical Evolution," 16–17; Howard Markel, "Case Shined First Light on Abuse of Children," *New York Times*, December 14, 2009, http://www.nytimes.com/2009/12/15/health/15abus.html (accessed November 3, 2017).

9 Rymph, *Raising Government Children*, 27.

10 *M'Lain v. Elder*, quoted in Pamela Bridgewater and Daina Ramey Berry, "Pregnancy," in *Enslaved Women in America: An Encyclopedia*,

horrors of Black enslavement in America and its aftermath have yet to be authentically addressed by white culture in the United States. As the Black liberation theologian Courtney Hall Lee reminds us, "During the time of American slavery, Black children could be bought, sold, beaten, and raped as property."[11]

Even if the children of those enslaved were kept with the same enslaver, contact between parent and child could be limited. After childbirth, an enslaved woman would be sent back to work as soon as she was physically able. The historian Catherine Rymph explains, "A slave woman's productive labor was seen as more valuable than the labor of child-rearing. Thus it was often older, weak, or ill women (who could not perform harder labor) who were given the tasks of 'mothering.'"[12] This resulted in children being raised by a community of enslaved adults and older children. Many scholars argue this form of child-rearing reinforced "the more expansive notions of kinship that West Africans brought with them to the America" and which to a large extent continue to this day in many African American families.[13]

After the Civil War, the Black Codes of the South permitted Black children to be deemed vagrants and appointed as apprentices, often to their former enslavers. Few orphanages in the North accepted African American children, and those that did faced additional difficulties. Orphanages for Black children in Philadelphia and New York were burned down by white mobs in 1838 and 1863, respectively.[14] But even in 1923, when 1,070 child welfare

---

ed. Daina Ramey Berry and Deleso A. Alford (Santa Barbara, CA: Greenwood, 2012).

11 Courtney Hall Lee, *Black Madonna: A Womanist Look at Mary of Nazareth* (Eugene, OR: Cascade Books, 2017), xii.

12 Rymph, *Raising Government Children*, 35.

13 Rymph, *Raising Government Children*, 35.

14 Don Lash, *"When the Welfare People Come": Race and Class in the US Child Protection System* (Chicago: Haymarket Books, 2017), 31–33;

agencies existed in northern states, 35 served only Black children, 264 accepted all races, 60 accepted nonwhite children who were not Black, and 711 served only white children.[15] Rymph observes that during the late nineteenth and first half of the twentieth centuries, "segregation laws and the indifference of white legislators and child welfare agencies meant that dependent Black children, especially in the South, were likely to end up in jail or reform school even when not charged with a crime because of the lack of more appropriate services."[16]

African American children began entering the child welfare system in greater numbers during the Great Migration (1910–1970). The Great Migration was a decades-long migration in which millions of Black families fled the South and settled in northern or West Coast cities.[17] During the 1950s, most foster parents were white, and welfare agencies had trouble placing Black children. There were several campaigns launched at this time to attract African American foster parents and increase the willingness of white families to host Black foster children.[18] From 1945 to 1961, the number of Black children in the child welfare system almost doubled, from 14 to 27 percent of children in the child welfare system.[19] It was during the early 1960s that the number of minority children in foster care began to be greater than their general proportion in the population.[20] During the post–World War II period, many civil rights activists blamed racial discrimination for the lack of CPS resources being offered to

---

McGowan, "Historical Evolution of Child Welfare Services," 14; Rymph, *Raising Government Children*, 35.

15 Dorothy Roberts, *Shattered Bonds: The Color of Child Welfare* (New York: Basic *Civitas* Book, 2002), 7.

16 Rymph, *Raising Government Children*, 36.

17 Lash, *"When the Welfare People Come,"* 38.

18 Rymph, *Raising Government Children*, 12–13.

19 Roberts, *Shattered Bonds*, 7.

20 Rymph, *Raising Government Children*, 130.

African American communities.[21] It should be remembered that CPS services during this period were largely voluntary. Though families sometimes felt coerced into decisions, most were not technically forced to place their children in foster care, and termination of parental rights was uncommon.[22]

Reflecting on the history of American slavery and the current CPS system, Dorothy Roberts comments, "Although most histories of the US child welfare system start with the charitable organizations founded in the 1800s to rescue poor white children, we can trace its origins back to slavery's control over Black families."[23] This is a provocative statement, but it is worth considering. Roberts's assertion is strengthened when one considers the Black Codes after the Civil War, which permitted the legal abduction of Black children from their homes to be placed in an apprenticeship in the home of a white family. Roberts convincingly states this is the "historical bridge" that connects slavery with the current foster care system.[24] As will be scrutinized later in this chapter, foster care was largely a voluntary option for families until the 1960s, when Black children became disproportionately represented in the foster care system.

CHILD WELFARE DURING THE EARLY TWENTIETH CENTURY

During the early twentieth century, there were around 1,500 orphanages serving over 140,000 children. Since many children entered these orphanages because of poverty, most of them had at least one living parent. Therefore, adoption was not common, and the biological parents of the children still

21 Rymph, *Raising Government Children*, 125.
22 Rymph, *Raising Government Children*, 119.
23 Roberts, *Torn Apart*, 90.
24 Roberts, *Torn Apart*, 97.

retained legal rights.[25] It was not until the latter half of the twentieth century that the termination of parental rights and adoption became more common. Before that, most children in foster care were either returned to their biological parents or remained in out-of-home care until they turned eighteen.[26]

At the beginning of the twentieth century, there was a growing appreciation of childhood development, which coincided with a belief that placing children in institutions was harmful to their development. Along with the publicized abuses at many private institutions and the growing notion that the protection of children was the responsibility of the state, the US Children's Bureau was established in 1912. The mandate for the bureau was broad and established a powerful role for the federal government in overseeing the life of children in the United States.[27]

This bureau was an outgrowth of the 1909 White House Conference on Children, which was convened by President Theodore Roosevelt. A strong sentiment from the conference was that poverty should not be the reason for family separations and that most children were best served by staying in their homes. Shortly afterward, twenty-one states passed legislation to offer financial aid to indigent parents who may have previously had their children removed.[28] The 1909 conference and the resulting legislation were almost exclusively concerned with white families, particularly European immigrant populations in the Northeast and Midwest. Ignored was the poverty faced by African American, Mexican, and

25 Rymph, *Raising Government Children*, 3.

26 Rymph, *Raising Government Children*, 95.

27 McGowan, "Historical Evolution," 19–20; US Statutes, session 2, chapter 73, section 2, April 9, 1912; Andrew L. Yarrow, "History of US Children's Policy: 1900 to Present," *First Focus*, April 2009, 2–3, https://firstfocus.org/wp-content/uploads/2014/06/Childrens-Policy-History.pdf (accessed August 28, 2020).

28 McGowan, "Historical Evolution," 23; Yarrow, "History of US Children's Policy," 2.

Native families. Catherine Rymph notes that "in a number of states with especially high African American and Mexican populations, little use was made of mothers' pensions at all, essentially preventing such families from receiving public support."[29]

Title IV of the Social Security Act of 1935 played a defining role for modern child welfare programs. Title IV, Aid to Dependent Children (ADC), which would eventually become Aid to Families with Dependent Children (AFDC), created a program that provided matching federal funds for impoverished families. The legislation required states to administer the program but provided flexibility for states in choosing how to operate and disperse funds.[30] Just before the passage of this legislation, there were 230,000 children benefiting from states' mothers' pensions and 102,577 children in official foster care homes. During this difficult time of the Great Depression, there were also eight million children under the age of sixteen whose families were receiving emergency relief.[31]

States could obtain ADC funding for keeping children with parents as well as providing more support for out-of-home care. The consequence of this legislation was the creation and strengthening of welfare and child welfare programs all over the country, especially in places where services had previously been scant or nonexistent.[32] It also led to a shift from children being removed from single mothers to supporting single mothers with children—at least that was the hope and intention of the reformers.[33]

29 Rymph, *Raising Government Children*, 28–29, 31.

30 Social Security Act of 1935, P. L. No. 74–271; McGowan, "Historical Evolution," 26; Rymph, *Raising Government Children*, 59.

31 Rymph, *Raising Government Children*, 45–46, 54.

32 Social Security Act of 1935, P. L. No. 74–271; McGowan, "Historical Evolution," 26.

33 McGowan, "Historical Evolution," 27.

The historian Catherine E. Rymph argues that "the assumptions and prejudices concerning class, gender, race, family, and welfare that kept many families outside the web of New Deal family security left foster care as the only option for the children of those families."[34] For example, an underlying assumption of the legislation was that the man was the breadwinner in a family and the woman was dependent on him. Therefore, a qualified widow could receive Old Age and Survivor's Insurance benefits that were more generous than those for single mothers, who only qualified for ADC. And since states could largely decide who qualified for benefits, most southern states configured the qualifications to exclude single Black mothers from ADC benefits.[35]

The unemployment rate peaked during the Great Depression at 25 percent in 1933. The creation of ADC during the 1930s helped ameliorate the poverty faced by families during this time. With the boost to the US economy brought on by World War II during the early 1940s, the unemployment rate dropped to just over 1 percent in 1944. Perhaps surprisingly, this change did not decrease the need for foster care. In 1941, there were 1.4 million women working in war industries. By the end of the war, this number increased to 5.5 million. With many fathers in the military and mothers working, there was no one home to watch the children. Some corporations offered daycare, and the federal government began funding daycare on a small scale, but the need was greater than the resources being offered. Many families placed their children in foster care as their only viable option in the face of inadequate daycare. Although some families were able to work out agreements with foster parents to only watch their children during the day (also known as foster daycare), many others had to place their children in

34 Rymph, *Raising Government Children*, 10.
35 Rymph, *Raising Government Children*, 60–61.

regular foster care until the father returned from the war or the mother was no longer working.[36]

CHILD WELFARE AFTER WORLD WAR II

After World War II, during the late 1940s and 1950s, it was believed by many in the child welfare field that poverty was no longer the reason for children entering foster care. The low unemployment of the war years had led to the false conclusion that the primary reason for child maltreatment was to be found in family pathologies. This included the belief that not only was there something likely damaged about the parents (e.g., alcoholic father or a mother with psychosis) but the children had probably developed emotional problems. Though almost all families that became involved with CPS during this time were living in poverty, most professionals were blind to recognizing poverty as a primary factor.[37] It was during this period that the concepts of family pathology and "hard-to-place" children became standardized. At first, these terms were applied to families of all races that lived in poverty, but by the late 1950s, they were used more often to describe the conditions surrounding African American families.[38]

The 1960s saw a tidal change in which foster care went from ideally being a voluntary service for struggling families to a system that was coercive and punitive.[39] This change was in large part due to the publication of *Children in Need of Parents*.[40] In Rymph's words, "This study exploded important

---

36 Rymph, *Raising Government Children*, 69, 75–78.
37 Rymph, *Raising Government Children*, 113–17.
38 Rymph, *Raising Government Children*, 113.
39 Rymph, *Raising Government Children*, 157–58.
40 Henry S. Maas and Richard E. Engler Jr., *Children in Need of Parents* (New York: Columbia University Press, 1959).

myths about modern foster care."[41] The first was that foster care was temporary. The study discovered that around a quarter million children were lingering in foster care for years at a time.[42] The study also made clear that poverty was still the primary factor in determining whose children entered foster care. It found that families who were disproportionately having their children placed in foster care were from those communities with the least accessibility to antipoverty programs.[43] Instead of ensuring greater access to antipoverty programs, the response was to place more emphasis on adoption and permanency.[44] Permanency, which will be covered below, tries to limit the number of out-of-home placements for children and find a permanent solution in the shortest period possible.

The publication of this book coincided with more Black mothers receiving welfare funds in the wake of the early civil rights movement. As Dorothy Roberts phrases it, CPS "policies took a dramatic turn for the worse as Southern states waged a backlash against the civil rights rebellion and Black mothers' claims to public aid. States began to punish poor mothers who failed to meet suitable-home standards by separating them from their children."[45] By 1960, Tennessee and Florida had enacted new laws in which welfare mothers whose homes did not meet certain standards were pressured to put their children in the custody of relatives or be charged with neglect. In 1960, welfare workers in Florida challenged the home conditions of thirteen thousand families, only 9 percent of whom were white.[46]

In 1961, amendments to the Social Security Act permitted AFDC payments to licensed foster parents. Perhaps the

41 Rymph, *Raising Government Children*, 158.
42 Rymph, *Raising Government Children*, 158–59.
43 Rymph, *Raising Government Children*, 160.
44 Rymph, *Raising Government Children*, 158–59.
45 Roberts, *Torn Apart*, 117.
46 Roberts, *Torn Apart*, 117.

most troubling part of this legislation was that these funds could only be used for foster care placements that were involuntary. Prior to this law, the majority of foster care placements were voluntary, but if states wanted to access these federal funds, there was now an incentive to create more coercive relationships with biological parents. Therefore, the 1960s witnessed increasing incidents of parents seeking help from CPS agencies, only to have their children involuntarily removed by court order. In addition, some CPS agencies began refusing to accept children into foster care on a voluntary basis. The funds were no longer there to pay for these voluntary services.[47]

Moreover, adult relatives who took in maltreated children were not eligible for foster care payments. If adult relatives were in financial difficulty, they would have to apply for AFDC welfare payments. Even if they were licensed foster care parents, they would have to settle for the AFDC payments, which were lower than foster care payments. Relatives who were licensed did finally begin to receive payments equal to other licensed parents after the Supreme Court case *Miller v. Youakim* (1979).[48]

By the early 1970s, the detrimental effects of these laws and practices on Black families were being noticed. In 1972, Andrew Billingsley and Jeanne M. Giovannoni published their influential *Children of the Storm: Black Children and American Child Welfare.*[49] The authors attacked the increasingly prevalent view that CPS agencies were "rescuing" Black children by removing them from their families and

47 Rymph, *Raising Government Children*, 170–71.

48 Marian S. Harris and Ada Skyles, "Kinship Care for African American Children," in *Child Maltreatment*, ed. John E. B. Myers (Los Angeles: Sage, 2012), 36–37.

49 Andrew Billingsley and Jeanne M. Giovannoni, *Children of the Storm: Black Children and American Child Welfare* (New York: Harcourt, 1972); Rymph, *Raising Government Children*, 172.

letting them languish in foster care with the hope that a better home would soon be found.[50]

In 1968, the National Association of Black Social Workers (NABSW) was formed by a group of social workers dissatisfied with the largest national group of social workers. The NABSW is best known for its 1972 statement taking a "vehement stand against the placement of Black children in white homes for any reason."[51] The statement spoke of how the white adoption of Black children cuts those children off from their cultural roots. It asserted that the practice of transracial adoption came from a shortage of white children for middle-class white parents to adopt, not from an "altruistic human concern for Black children."[52] When Black children legitimately needed to be removed from their home, it advocated for placement with relatives or adoption by Black families, whom the association believed had not been adequately recruited.[53]

Many of the concerns expressed by the NABSW are still relevant today. Dr. Patricia McManus, president and CEO of the Black Health Coalition of Wisconsin, relates the trouble that often arises when young African American children—who were adopted by white families in the suburbs or rural areas—reach their teenage years. She explains that it is between the ages of eleven and fifteen when children develop their "external identity." For Black children in almost exclusively white environments, this can be a time of deep isolation. This isolation takes on greater implications because their white adoptive parents cannot provide

50 Rymph, *Raising Government Children*, 172.

51 National Association of Black Social Workers, "Position Statement on Trans-Racial Adoptions," 1972, https://cdn.ymaws.com/www.nabsw.org/resource/resmgr/position_statements_papers/nabsw_trans-racial_adoption_.pdf (accessed November 26, 2019).

52 National Association of Black Social Workers, "Position Statement."

53 National Association of Black Social Workers, "Position Statement."

firsthand advice on how a Black person can navigate a white racist environment.

Around 2015, McManus met with five district attorneys from different parts of Wisconsin who shared concerns with her from white parents who did not know how to support and nurture a Black adopted child's growing external identity. These district attorneys had been accosted by white parents who had adopted young Black children, but these children were now acting out as teenagers in response to the white hostility they were facing in their mostly white communities. The parents were wondering if the children could be returned to their biological parents, which was also the desire of the children. This is not allowed in Wisconsin, but it has been permitted elsewhere. McManus is certain this request is quite common in the State of Wisconsin, but it is impossible to know how common because the number of requests is not tracked.[54]

Even though the number of orphans dropped dramatically by the 1960s, the number of children in foster care increased from 73,000 in 1923 to 177,000 by 1962. A major factor in the increase was a shift in child welfare from serving orphans to neglected children.[55] In addition, starting in the mid-1960s and before the end of the 1970s, every state passed mandatory reporting laws.[56] The Catholic sociologist and lawyer Stephen M. Krason cites this period in the 1970s as the beginning of modern CPS. In January 1974, Congress passed the Child Abuse Prevention and Treatment Act (CAPTA), also called the Mondale Act after its main senate sponsor, the future vice president Walter F. Mondale.

54 Patricia McManus, "Speech at International Women's Day Celebration" (speech, Milwaukee, WI, March 8, 2020).

55 Lindsey, *The Welfare of Children*, 27–28; Tobis, *From Pariahs to Partners*, 2.

56 Lois Weinberg, *The Systematic Mistreatment of Children in the Foster Care System* (New York: Routledge, 2007), 2; Child Abuse Prevention and Treatment Act of 1974, Pub. L. No. 93–247.

This legislation created greater uniformity among states and required mandated reporting by many professionals for "even *suspected* cases of child abuse and neglect." In return, the federal government began pouring large sums of money into states' budgets for child welfare services.[57]

Mandatory reporters can include medical professionals, teachers, daycare providers, law enforcement, social workers, public housing workers, the juvenile court system, and shelters for homeless people. For these workers, suspected child maltreatment must be reported under threat of criminal or civil penalties.[58] Sixty-five percent of alleged reports of child maltreatment are made by professionals who come into contact with the family as part of their job.[59] Regarding their mandatory reporting responsibilities, 71 percent of physicians and nurses state that identifying child abuse or neglect is rather difficult or difficult. Part of this difficulty is related to the fact that evidence-based standards for discerning child maltreatment are few, and the ones that exist are greatly lacking in specificity. This results in the physicians and nurses having to make extremely subjective decisions when determining if there is reasonable cause to suspect that a child in their care is a victim of maltreatment.[60] Although it is difficult to find national data on child maltreatment reports by race, California has recent data. In 2018, CPS agencies in California received a report of child maltreatment on 43.4 of every 1,000

57 Stephen M. Krason, "The Mondale Act and Its Aftermath," in *Child Abuse, Family Rights, and the Child Protective System*, ed. Stephen M. Krason (Lanham: Scarecrow Press, 2013), 1–81, on p. 1. Emphasis in the original.

58 Weinberg, *Systematic Mistreatment of Children*, 2; Child Abuse Prevention and Treatment Act of 1974, Pub. L. No. 93–247.

59 McGowan, "Historical Evolution," 32.

60 Brett Drake et al., "Racial Bias in Child Protection? A Comparison of Competing Explanations Using National Data," *Pediatrics* 127, no. 3 (March 2011): 2, https://pdfs.semanticscholar.org/8f38/1035aca3a26ea274091abc8af079dce57c3c.pdf (accessed August 6, 2019).

white children and on 124.3 of every 1,000 Black children.[61] That means that child-maltreatment reports against Black children occurred almost three times as often compared to white children based on their respective populations.

The 1967 Social Security Amendments also resulted in increased funding and expansion of CPS services. In addition, state and local governments were now permitted to purchase services from private organizations.[62] The combination of mandatory reporting laws and the Social Security Amendments of 1967 resulted in a massive increase in the number of CPS employees. In 1955, there were just over five thousand full-time CPS employees in the United States. Within ten years, this number doubled; by 1976, there were over thirty thousand full-time employees. Krason believes these developments have resulted in an atmosphere where far too many parents have been unjustly harassed or had their children unjustly removed.[63]

It was during this period in the 1960s and 1970s that we see the professionalization and standardization of child welfare services. As the historian Catherine E. Rymph states, "Foster care services as they existed in the 1930s did not yet constitute a 'system,' neither a professional, efficient, caring one nor an anonymous, heartless, dysfunctional one. Foster care was instead provided haphazardly through a tangle of practices with roots in much earlier efforts of public authorities, charities, entrepreneurs, and private families."[64]

---

61 "Reports of Child Abuse and Neglect, by Race/Ethnicity," KidsData, https://www.kidsdata.org/topic/3/reported-abuse-race/table#fmt=1217&loc=2&tf=108&ch=7,11,8,10,9&sortColumnId=0&sortType=asc (accessed March 7, 2021).

62 McGowan, "Historical Evolution," 32.

63 Lindsey, *Welfare of Children*, 19–20; Krason, "Mondale Act and Its Aftermath," 1–2; Children's Bureau, *Child Maltreatment 2016: Summary of Key Findings*, July 2018, 2, https://www.childwelfare.gov/pubPDFs/canstats.pdf (accessed September 21, 2018).

64 Rymph, *Raising Government Children*, 2–3.

CHILD WELFARE AND THE WAR ON DRUGS

In 1980, the Adoption Assistance and Child Welfare Act passed, which stressed providing services to keep children in their homes. If out-of-home placement was deemed necessary, children were to be placed as close as possible to the parents, and the priority was on reunification. Stressing the need for permanency in the lives of children, the act held that foster care was to be avoided and adoption more quickly completed when staying with or returning to the family was not an option.[65] This legislation did not fulfill its intended purpose. Between 1977 and 1994, the number of children being served by CPS while staying in their homes decreased from two million to one million.[66] From 1982 to 1999, the number of children in foster care doubled, and the number of Black children entering foster care soared as the War on Drugs led to more police contact in poor urban areas.[67] Currently, law enforcement is a close second to teachers in the number of suspected child-maltreatment reports they convey to CPS agencies. Because of the high standing of police among many in US society, their reports are given more credibility and are more likely to lead to a substantiated case of child maltreatment in a which a child is labeled a victim than other reports.[68]

By 1995, half of all child victims "involved a caregiver alleged to be chemically dependent."[69] In addition, studies from that time document that the lopsided application of drug testing on birthing mothers occurred "almost exclusively

65 McGowan, "Historical Evolution," 36–37; Harris and Skyles, "Kinship Care," 34–46, on p. 37.

66 Roberts, *Shattered Bonds*, 15. Although this source is a little older, it is still relevant. Additionally, Roberts is one of the few scholars to confront anti-Blackness in CPS.

67 Roberts, *Shattered Bonds*, 8; Lash, *"When the Welfare People Come,"* 40.

68 Roberts, *Torn Apart*, 192, 194.

69 Lash, *"When the Welfare People Come,"* 40.

at public hospitals that served poor communities of color."[70] The Black liberation theologian Kelly Brown Douglas states that "the War on Drugs served its purpose. It has returned unprecedented numbers of Black bodies to a chattel space—the new plantation of jails and prisons." It is no coincidence the United States imprisons a greater percentage of its racial minorities than any other country in the world.[71]

The use of the War on Drugs to incarcerate Blacks in the wake of the freedoms that African Americans had attained during the civil rights movement repeated an old strategy. After Black slaves had been freed in the South following the end of the Civil War, many southern states enacted Black Codes, which permitted Blacks to be jailed and utilized for free labor for minor offenses, such as loitering. But as John Derek Stern notes, the War on Drugs was "not exclusive to the South but throughout the entire United States."[72] The War on Drugs during the 1980s played an integral role in preparing the United States for the onslaught of laws in the 1990s to further attack the Black family. Michelle Alexander observes that as of 2009, there were "nearly 7.3 million people currently under correctional control, only 1.6 million are in prison."[73] The other 5.7 million people who are under "correctional control" are on probation and parole—mostly for nonviolent offenses, and they are disproportionately Black. This results in more contact with government authorities, which increases the odds of one's family becoming involved with CPS.

70 Roberts, *Torn Apart*, 2.

71 Kelly Brown Douglas, *Stand Your Ground* (Maryknoll, NY: Orbis Books, 2015), 128–29.

72 John Derek Stern, "The War on Drugs and Jim Crow's the Most Wanted: A Social and Historical Look at Mass Incarceration," *Ramapo Journal of Law and Society*, June 15, 2017, https://www.ramapo.edu/law-journal/thesis/war-drugs-jim-crows-wanted-social-historical-look-mass-incarceration/ (accessed March 11, 2019).

73 Alexander, *New Jim Crow*, 101–2.

To put the disenfranchisement of Black Americans and the lack of involved Black fathers into perspective, Michelle Alexander laments:

> More Black men are imprisoned today than at any other moment in our nation's history. More are disenfranchised today than in 1870, the year the Fifteenth Amendment was ratified prohibiting laws that explicitly deny the right to vote on the basis of race. Young Black men today may be just as likely to suffer discrimination in employment, housing, public benefits, and jury service as a Black man in the Jim Crow era—discrimination that is perfectly legal, because it is based on one's criminal record.[74]

RACISM AND POLITICS DURING THE 1990S

The mid-1990s saw the passage of three laws that disproportionately affected impoverished Black families. The first, the Multiethnic Placement Act of 1994 (MEPA), prohibited CPS agencies receiving federal funding from delaying or denying a foster care or adoption placement solely on the basis of race. In 1996, Congress would strengthen the bill to prevent race from being a factor at all. The legal scholar and sociologist Dorothy Roberts's summary of contemporary news coverage reveals that the legislative purpose of this law was to allow the adoption of Black children by white parents. Before the passage of the law, only 1–4 percent of adoptions involved Black children being adopted by white parents.[75] Current information is extremely difficult to find, but the psychologist researcher Nicholas Zill estimates that

74 Alexander, *New Jim Crow*, 180–81.
75 Roberts, *Shattered Bonds*, 165–72.

55 percent of Black adoptees are raised by parents of another race.[76] In contrast, white children are adopted by parents of color only 3 percent of the time.[77]

The second law was the Welfare Reform Act of 1996, which placed a five-year lifetime limit on welfare benefits and lowered the monetary benefit while requiring the mother to work to receive funds. Although the original intent of welfare was to keep children with their single mothers, welfare reform made this more difficult. At the very least, a mother would be required to work at what was likely a low-wage job while placing her children in daycare. Roberts argues this law could be passed because the "public devalues Black mothers' work in particular because it sees these mothers as inherently unfit and even affirmatively harmful to their children."[78]

Roberts observes that welfare supports the unity of the biological family when white mothers are involved but exerts punishment and separation of families when African Americans are involved.[79] While welfare reform laws were being implemented in the 1990s, judges and CPS workers explained that the lack of a safety net for families living in poverty would result in the disappearance of "the blurry line between destitution and neglect."[80] In addition, welfare reform gave states greater flexibility in how they used federal

76 Nicholas Zill, "The Changing Face of Adoption in the United States," *Institute for Family Studies*, August 8, 2017, https://ifstudies.org/blog/the-changing-face-of-adoption-in-the-united-states (accessed December 27, 2018).

77 Sarah Catherine Williams, "State-Level Data for Understanding Child Welfare in the United States," Child Trends, February 28, 2022, https://www.childtrends.org/publications/state-level-data-for-understanding-child-welfare-in-the-united-states (accessed March 5, 2023).

78 Roberts, *Shattered Bonds*, 179.

79 Roberts, *Shattered Bonds*, 172–81.

80 Nina Bernstein, "Welfare Cuts to Swamp Foster Care System," *Wisconsin State Journal*, November 21, 1995, 5B.

welfare dollars. As of 2020, forty-two states divert some of these funds to CPS, with twelve states diverting more than 20 percent of their welfare dollars to CPS.[81]

In the mid-1980s, the Reagan administration began pushing the myth that welfare payments were an "incentive" for impoverished families—particularly Black families—to have more children. The Black political activist and academic Angela Davis noted at the time that while the percentage of Black babies born to single mothers had increased to 55 percent in 1985, Black teenage birth rates remained the same from 1920 to 1990. The perceived increase in births to single Black women was due to older married Black women having fewer children—a trend that began in the 1960s and 1970s. Leading up to the midterm elections in 1994, Republican commentators again promoted the false connection between welfare and an increase in births to single Black mothers. This strategy helped Republicans gain control of both houses of Congress and was influential in selling the public on the needs for so-called welfare reform.[82]

The third law was the Adoption and Safe Families Act of 1997 (ASFA), which emphasizes child safety over preserving the unity of the biological family. It also encourages the quick termination of parental rights if parents are not able to quickly resolve CPS concerns and follow CPS guidelines. In most instances, a petition to terminate parental rights must be filed when a child has been in out-of-home care for fifteen of the last twenty-two months. Dorothy Roberts argues that the limited foster care timeline places an undue burden on

81 Diana Azevedo-McCaffrey and Ali Safawi, "Policy Brief: To Promote Equity, States Should Invest More TANF Dollars in Basic Assistance," Center on Budget and Policy Priorities, January 12, 2022, 7, https://www.cbpp.org/sites/default/files/atoms/files/1-10-17tanf.pdf (accessed March 6, 2023).

82 Kendi, *Stamped from the Beginning*, 438–39, 452.

parents whose "children spend too long in foster care because of unreasonable demands placed on their parents or delays caused by the child welfare agency."[83]

In 1999, the number of children in out-of-home care peaked at 567,000. By 2012, it had declined 30 percent to 397,000. But it is has since increased and stabilized at around 430,000. Between 1998 and 2002, yearly adoptions from foster care in the United States increased from thirty-six thousand to fifty-one thousand and then stabilized.[84] Essentially, ASFA had the intended effect of lowering the number of children in out-of-home care by increasing the number of adoptions.

ASFA also provided a financial incentive to states that increased the number of foster children who were adopted. States would receive four thousand dollars for each child adopted over and above the state's base rate of foster care adoptions. This base rate is determined by the lesser of either the number of children adopted the previous year or the average number of children adopted during the previous three years. An additional two thousand dollars was provided for states that increased the adoptions of special-needs children.[85]

---

83 Roberts, *Shattered Bonds*, 151; Children's Bureau, *The AFCARS Report*, no. 28, 3.

84 Jill Duerr Berrick, "Trends and Issues in the US Child Welfare System," in *Child Protection Systems: International Trends and Orientations*, ed. Neil Gilbert, Nigel Parton, and Marit Skivenes (New York: Oxford University Press, 2011), 27. I confirmed that the annual average of foster care adoptions has been around fifty thousand through the US Children's Bureau reports available at https://www.acf.hhs.gov/cb/research-data-technology/statistics-research/afcars.

85 Lauren R. Shapiro and Marie-Helen Maras, *Multidisciplinary Investigation of Child Maltreatment* (Burlington, MA: Jones and Bartlett Learning, 2016), 283; US Administration for Children and Families, "Program Instruction on Adoption and Legal Guardianship Incentive Payments," Log No: ACYF-CB-PI-15-08, July 8, 2015, https://www.acf.hhs.gov/cb/policy-guidance/pi-15-08 (accessed March 6, 2023).

The 2008 law Fostering Connections to Success and Increasing Adoptions amended the 1997 legislation to provide states with four thousand-dollar incentives for each child adopted above a state's adoption numbers for 2002. If the child is over nine years old, the incentive increases to eight thousand dollars. Essentially, this legislation shifted the emphasis from family preservation to adoption.[86] This law has since been amended, and states now receive five thousand dollars for each foster care adoption for each young child (ages zero to eight) above a state's base rate. States receive seventy-five hundred dollars for each preadolescent (ages nine to thirteen) child adoption increase and ten thousand dollars for each child adoption over the age of thirteen.[87]

Lash believes that racism, even if unintentional, played a role in passing the 1990s legislation. He argues that it would never be viewed as better for middle-class white children to be separated from their parents. The assumption in the American psyche is that most child victims are removed from impoverished Black parents.[88] And this vision of ASFA makes it acceptable to most white Americans. Roberts boldly asserts that Congress's intent with the permanency rules of ASFA was "terminating the rights of Black parents, not reducing poverty or building strong support for families."[89]

86 McGowan, "Historical Evolution," 39–40; Adoption and Safe Families Act of 1997, Pub. L. No. 105–89; Roberts, *Shattered Bonds*, 150–51; Berrick, "Trends and Issues," 23, 27; Fostering Connections to Success and Increasing Adoptions Act of 2008 (HR 6893), Social Security Act Title IV, Part E, Sec. 473A, https://www.ssa.gov/OP_Home/ssact/title04/0473A.htm#ft258 (accessed November 14, 2017).

87 Fostering Connections to Success and Increasing Adoptions Act of 2008 (HR 6893), Social Security Act Title IV, Part E, Sec. 473A, https://www.ssa.gov/OP_Home/ssact/title04/0473A.htm#ft258 (accessed November 14, 2017).

88 Lash, *"When the Welfare People Come,"* 26.

89 Roberts, *Shattered Bonds*, 164.

Roberts contends that the passage of these three laws in the mid-1990s was an orchestrated assault on the Black family. Each successive law made it more difficult for impoverished Black mothers to raise their children and easier for CPS to adopt their children out to white families.[90]

There were additional changes in federal spending priorities during the Clinton administration that adversely affected families living in poverty. By 1996, twice as much money from the federal budget was spent on prisons than welfare. The public housing budget was cut by 61 percent (a seventeen-billion-dollar decrease), and the prison budget was increased by 171 percent (a nineteen-billion-dollar increase). Federal expenditures for foster care increased by 30 percent in the late 1990s, while food stamps were cut by 33 percent, and welfare benefits were decreased by 19 percent. As Michelle Alexander notes, Clinton did not lower the funding spent on the "urban poor" during his administration as much as he "was radically altering what the funds would be used for."[91]

FAMILY FIRST PREVENTION SERVICES ACT OF 2018 AND TODAY

Since the 1990s, there have not been any major changes to federal law regarding CPS. Billions of dollars continue to pour into the business of child welfare. The Health and Human Services Administration for Children and Families has a budget of nearly ten billion dollars, most of which is used to support and monitor local CPS agencies. When state and local funds are taken into account, child welfare is a thirty-billion-dollar-a-year industry. When the twenty-three billion dollars per year spent on foster care is divided by

90 Roberts, *Shattered Bonds*, 165–66.

91 Alexander, *New Jim Crow*, 57; Roberts, *Torn Apart*, 122–23.

the number of children in foster care, we find that it costs approximately fifty-seven thousand dollars per year for each child placement. Between cuts to welfare and increased funding for foster care, there were seven states in 2018 that had more children in foster care than children being supported in their homes with the help of Temporary Assistance for Needy Families (TANF) benefits (or welfare).[92]

In 2018, we saw the passage of the Family First Prevention Services Act (FFPSA), which aims to funnel more money into preventative services. This was a bipartisan effort that had the explicit purpose of "keeping children safely with their families to avoid the trauma that results when children are placed in out-of-home care." This legislation has not diverted money to families in need but rather to service providers in the areas of mental health, substance-use treatment, and improved parenting skills. It is also supposed to make courts less confrontational and more focused on advocating for solutions that would preserve families when possible.[93] As Dorothy Roberts observes, this only increases government monitoring of Black and impoverished families without providing them with any increased support for their "material needs."[94]

On the practical level, the family advocate Amada Morales has seen this money used by private foster care agencies in Milwaukee County to create and fill advocate positions, but she has not seen these advocates play a substantial role in changing how social workers treat families with open CPS cases.[95] Even before the passage of the FFPSA, private agencies across the country had been accessing the bloated

92 Roberts, *Torn Apart*, 142, 145.

93 US Children's Bureau, "Family First Prevention Services Act," Child Welfare Information Gateway, n.d., https://www.childwelfare.gov/topics/systemwide/laws-policies/federal/family-first/ (accessed March 15, 2022).

94 Roberts, *Torn Apart*, 144–45.

95 Amada Morales, interview by author, Milwaukee, WI, March 16, 2022.

federal CPS budget in the name of providing services to "at-risk" families. This increased supervision of Black and impoverished families by CPS-funded agencies actually raises the chances that one may lose one's children if the agency becomes concerned. Essentially, the FFPSA confirmed a practice that was already happening and did not make any serious changes that would help families out of poverty or prevent children from being removed from their homes.

Within the context of these laws, the liberty of Black parents was—and continues to be—impugned in US society. By *liberty*, I mean the free will that parents should have in making choices about raising their children. Their options have been limited by a society that provides fewer opportunities for quality housing, work, education, and healthcare to a large segment of the population. Your choices are limited if the father of your child has a statistically increased chance of being arrested or sent to prison for a disproportionately longer period than a white father. (For example, Black people in Wisconsin are twelve times more likely to be sent to prison than white people.)[96] If you are more likely to have interactions with CPS because you are African American—and there are white suburban families waiting in line to adopt your child—your liberty and free will are impugned.

THE CONSTITUTION AND THE SUPREME COURT

Although this book is not a legal text, a brief explanation of how courts in the United States have viewed the constitutionality of parental rights will help provide a more complete

96 Deon J. Hampton, "Wisconsin Leads Nation in Imprisonment Rates of Black People," *NBC News*, November 1, 2021, https://www.nbcnews.com/news/us-news/wisconsin-leads-nation-imprisonment-rates-black-people-rcna4160 (accessed December 11, 2021).

picture of the situation. Roberts notes that family rights are bestowed on Americans through their individual rights: "The U.S. Constitution doesn't mention families."[97] Parents can legally challenge the unwarranted removal of a child using the Fourth Amendment, which states the "right of the people to be secure in their person, houses, papers, and effects, against unreasonable searches and seizures, shall not be violated, and no Warrants shall issue, but upon probable cause, supported by Oath or affirmation, and particularly describing the place to be searched, and the persons or things to be seized." *Tenenbaum v. Williams* (1999) stated the Fourth Amendment required a court order to seize children if time allowed. Additionally, *Duchesne v. Sugarman* (1977) cited the same amendment, stating the "right of the family to remain together without the coercive interference of the awesome power of the state . . . [is] the most essential and basic aspect of family privacy."[98] Both of these were decisions made by separate US Courts of Appeals. Dorothy Roberts observes that the US Supreme Court has never ruled on whether "the Fourth Amendment's requirements of a particularized warrant and probable cause apply to child welfare investigations."[99]

The Fourteenth Amendment, which guarantees "no state shall deprive any person of life, liberty, or property without due process of the law," has been cited by the Supreme Court to protect the rights of parents in raising their children.[100] *Meyer v. Nebraska* (1923) stated the Fourteenth Amendment provided for the right to raise children. More recently, *Santosky v. Kramer* (1982) established that a parent must be proven to be unfit before the notion of the best interests of the child

97 Roberts, *Shattered Bonds*, 225.

98 Quoted in Shapiro and Maras, *Multidisciplinary Investigation*, 245–46.

99 Roberts, *Torn Apart*, 164.

100 Roberts, *Shattered Bonds*, 225. For example, *Meyer v. Nebraska* (1923) and *Pierce v. Society of Sisters* (1925).

can be employed to terminate parental rights.[101] Later in the chapter, we will examine the CPS process for allegations and see how these court rulings have translated into practice for families that come into contact with CPS.

UN CONVENTION ON THE RIGHTS OF A CHILD

To round out this legal topic, it may be helpful to note the basic international document on children's rights, the *United Nations Convention on the Rights of a Child* (UNCRD),[102] which was a treaty adopted by the United Nations in 1989 that has since been ratified by the majority of the world's countries, including the Vatican. The preamble and several articles of the declaration affirm the family as the fundamental unit in any society, which should be protected and aided so that parents have the tools to properly raise their children. The document specifically singles out the responsibility of the state to ensure adequate food, clothing, and housing for families. The declaration also promotes the primacy of the "best interests of the child" principle, though this term is never defined or described. It advocates the temporary or permanent removal of the child in cases of abuse or neglect if it is in the best interests of the child. Unfortunately, the declaration does not address situations when neglect can be attributed to a society's lack of support for the family.[103]

When it is deemed best to place a child in foster care or to have the child adopted, the declaration urges "continuity

101 Roberts, *Shattered Bonds*, 227–28.

102 United Nations, General Assembly, *United Nations Convention on the Rights of a Child,* November 20, 1989, https://www.ohchr.org/en/professionalinterest/pages/crc.aspx (accessed July 3, 2020).

103 United Nations, General Assembly, *United Nations Convention on the Rights of a Child.*

in a child's upbringing and to the child's ethnic, religious, cultural and linguistic background."[104] For African Americans in the United States, this would indicate they should be placed with other African American families, but this principle has been completely ignored in the United States with regard to Black families since the mid-1990s.

The United States has signed the treaty but not ratified it, making it the only UN member state not to ratify the declaration. Theories for why the United States has not ratified it range from the treaty not being necessary to it infringing on the sovereignty of the country. Once a nation ratifies the treaty, it is required to submit regular reports and make changes in certain domestic laws to comply with it. For example, the United Kingdom set goals to lower child poverty as a result of ratifying the declaration.[105] Ratification of the declaration by the United States may lead to similar conversations about child poverty that many legislators would rather avoid.

CPS APPARATUS FOR PROCESSING ALLEGATIONS

Although policies and processes vary from state to state and county to county, this section will lay out the typical process of a child welfare case from beginning to end. Child welfare agencies begin a new case when they are contacted with an allegation of neglect or abuse. These allegations may come from mandated reporters or any person who suspects maltreatment has occurred. If the nature of the allegation fits

104 United Nations, General Assembly, *United Nations Convention on the Rights of a Child.*

105 United Nations, General Assembly, *United Nations Convention on the Rights of a Child*; Amy Rothschild, "Is America Holding Out on Protecting Children's Rights?" *Atlantic*, May 2, 2017, https://www.theatlantic.com/education/archive/2017/05/holding-out-on-childrens-rights/524652/ (accessed July 3, 2020).

the statutory definition of child maltreatment, an investigation will be opened. If the allegation does not meet the statutory definition, the case is closed. When an investigation is considered warranted, a CPS investigator interviews the alleged child victim, the primary caregivers, the person who made the accusation, and other relevant people. The process can take anywhere from a couple of hours to several months. Usually, the child is found to be in a safe situation, and the case is closed.

In 2020, there were 3.9 million referrals or allegations submitted to child welfare agencies throughout the United States. Of these, 54.2 percent met the criteria for an investigation; 29 percent of the investigated cases determined that the child was a victim—meaning the allegation of maltreatment against the child was substantiated. This means that 71 percent of investigated cases did not find credible evidence a child was living in an unsafe environment.[106] For an allegation to be substantiated during the initial assessment, there must be "a preponderance of evidence" that child maltreatment has occurred.[107] A preponderance of evidence indicates there is a greater weight of evidence that maltreatment occurred than it did not. It is the same legal standard required to win a civil suit but is a lower standard proof than required for criminal court.

It should be noted that decisions at this level vary widely among states. In 2020, confirmed child victims ranged from 1.7 child victims per 1,000 children in Pennsylvania to 19.0 child victims per 1,000 children in Maine.[108] In other words, a child in Maine is eleven times more likely to be considered

106 Children's Bureau of the US, *Child Maltreatment 2020*, x–xi.

107 Wisconsin Department of Children and Families, "Wisconsin Child Abuse and Neglect Report: Annual Report for Calendar Year 2015," 2.3, https://www.wistatedocuments.org/digital/api/collection/p267601coll4/id/14907/download (accessed March 22, 2023).

108 Children's Bureau of the US, *Child Maltreatment 2020*, 36.

a victim of child maltreatment than a child in Pennsylvania. To put it another way, a parent in Maine is eleven times more likely to be considered a perpetrator of child maltreatment than a parent in Pennsylvania. It is difficult to believe that the parents in Maine are that much worse than parents in Pennsylvania.

If it is determined that a parent engaged in behaviors that violate abuse and neglect laws, the investigator must decide if the child should be removed from the home or if setting up a safety plan with the parent will be satisfactory. Dorothy Roberts notes that safety plans are considered voluntary because parents agree to them outside of a court mandate. Nevertheless, parents are often coerced into safety plans under threat of having their children removed. In these situations, the caseworker has broad authority to disrupt the life of a family without any court oversight. In the words of one caseworker, "I have more power than the president of the United States. I can come to your house and take your children away."[109]

There is no uniform method for determining the risk to the child if they should remain at home. Methods can vary from an individual worker's judgment to a research-based structured decision-making tool. If the investigator believes the child cannot safely remain in the home, the child is moved to a relative, foster family, or another temporary shelter. Again, there is wide variation from state to state regarding how many children are removed from the home. The range of children in foster care during 2020 varied from 2.2 per 1,000 children in New Jersey to 19.0 per 1,000 children in West Virginia.[110] There is also wide variation concerning what percentage of children are reunified

109 Quoted in Roberts, *Torn Apart*, 134–35.

110 Weinberg, *Systematic Mistreatment of Children*, 3; Berrick, "Trends and Issues," 17–35, on pp. 21–22. This statistic was deduced from data from the Kids Count Data Center (https://datacenter.kidscount.org/), taking

with their biological parents. In 2019, the national average was 53.3 percent, with 23.7 percent of children being reunified in Delaware and 77.1 percent of children being reunified in South Carolina.[111]

Except in emergency situations, a CPS worker is supposed to obtain a warrant or a court order signed by a judge to proceed with removal. In many jurisdictions, CPS workers will bring police officers when confronting the family to state they are there to remove the child. It is surprisingly common for the CPS worker to do this without a warrant, but the intimidation factor of the police officer normally results in parents handing over their children. In Milwaukee and elsewhere, CPS workers have access to prestamped judges' orders, which the workers fill out themselves. This is not the appropriate way to obtain a court order. If a CPS investigator comes to the conclusion that the child is in a dangerous situation that cannot be rectified through in-home education or assistance, a warrant is supposed to be obtained with a judge's approval to place the child in out-of-home care.

On removal of the child from their home, the CPS agency must file a petition with the court listing the justification for removing jurisdiction of the child from the parents to the court. Normally, the petition must be filed within forty-eight hours of removal, with copies of the petition being served to each parent. Within seventy-two hours of removal, a detention and arraignment hearing should take place in court.[112] In some states, the petition is referred to as a Child in Need of Protective Services (CHIPS) petition. The hearings associated with the arraignment and the

into account total child population and total number of children in foster care in 2019 by state.

111 Children's Bureau, *Child Welfare Outcomes 2019: Report to Congress*, 30, 65, https://www.acf.hhs.gov/cb/report/cwo-2019 (accessed March 26, 2023). As this book went to press, these were the latest statistics available on reunification.

112 Weinberg, *Systematic Mistreatment of Children*, 4–6.

additional hearings to work toward reunification are called a *CHIPS case*.

Although the court setting varies by state, these proceedings normally take place in juvenile, family, or probate court.[113] At the arraignment hearing, the CPS agency will provide probable-cause evidence of maltreatment as well as cause for removal and temporary physical custody of the child. If the judge does not find the evidence to be convincing, the child will be returned to the family. When this happens, the case is either closed, or the child is sent home with a safety plan. If the judge agrees with CPS, decisions will be made about the details for out-of-home placement.[114]

Next, there will be an adjudication hearing, also known as the fact-finding hearing or jurisdictional hearing, in which the court decides if CPS can prove the child-maltreatment allegations. As preparations are being made for the hearing, pretrial negotiations or mediation may be used to reach a reunification agreement. If this happens, the agreement will serve as a plan toward reunification, follow-up, and the eventual closing of the case. If an agreement is not met, a full hearing takes place. During the adjudication hearing, lawyers for CPS, the parents, and the child may present evidence and witnesses. The burden is on CPS to prove child maltreatment. If the judge finds the evidence unconvincing, the child is returned, and the case is closed. If the judge upholds the allegations, the court takes jurisdiction of the child (meaning the court can make decisions about the permanent living situation for the child), and the judge will also state the exact problems that need to be resolved for reunification.[115]

Next, the judge will schedule a disposition hearing, the purpose of which is to determine permanent legal custody for the child, including any services to be provided for the child

113 Weinberg, *Systematic Mistreatment of Children*, 5.
114 Weinberg, *Systematic Mistreatment of Children*, 7.
115 Weinberg, *Systematic Mistreatment of Children*, 7.

and family. According to ASFA (1997), the judge must prioritize the safety of the child in deciding a permanent placement. Normally, if a child is reunified with the biological family or primary caregiver, there will be a safety plan set in place by the judge that must be followed. If the conditions are fulfilled, the case will be closed. If they are not, the judge will decide whether it is most appropriate to place the child with another relative, a foster home, a group home, or an adoptive family. If adoption is not an immediate option or a relative cannot continue to care for the child, review hearings are to be held every six months.[116] Of children placed in foster care, about 53 percent are reunified with their parents. Regardless, the average stay of a child in foster care is twenty-one months.

If there is a judicial determination that the child cannot be reunited with the parents or if a child is nearing twelve months in out-of-home care, a permanency hearing is scheduled. The purpose of this hearing is to make a final determination whether the child should be (1) reunited with family on a specific date, (2) placed for adoption, (3) placed permanently with a relative but with CPS retaining legal custody or the ultimate decision on where a child will live, (4) given permanent placement with a relative as legal guardian (where the relative is given legal custody of the child, but the parents may retain some rights, such as visitation and access to information), or (5) placed in another permanent setting.

Depending on what is viewed as in the best interests of the child, this hearing could include a petition for the termination of parental rights. When the court decides to terminate parental rights, finding a permanent placement can be very difficult for many children. Therefore, additional permanency hearings are to be held every twelve months until a permanent placement has been realized.[117]

116 Weinberg, *Systematic Mistreatment of Children*, 9–13.

117 Weinberg, *Systematic Mistreatment of Children*, 9–13; Children's Bureau, "Court Hearings for the Permanent Placement of Children,"

Since parents are not at risk of incarceration as in a criminal court case, the legal bar for terminating parental rights is lower. To obtain a guilty verdict in a criminal case, the evidence presented must prove beyond a reasonable doubt that criminal conduct was perpetrated by the defendant. Most courts that oversee the separation of children and the termination of parental rights only require a preponderance of evidence, which is a much lower standard that only requires there be "a greater than 50% chance that the claim is true."[118] This is the same standard used in civil trials. But most civil trials are about money, debts, or property—not losing one's right to raise and see one's child.

Although the United States enshrines certain rights in criminal cases, these same rights are not guaranteed on the federal level for parents since they are not criminal defendants. They only exist to the extent that the individual state enacts them. As the child welfare reformer David Tobis observes, "In at least 12 states, parents do not have an absolute statutory right to counsel after the initiation of child protection proceedings against them. In at least six states, parents do not have an absolute statutory right to counsel in termination of parental rights hearings."[119]

As will be further investigated, poverty plays an integral role in bringing families into contact with CPS. And once a family enters the CPS apparatus, poverty prevents parents from being able to hire their own lawyers. For states where a lawyer is not guaranteed for the entire CPS court process, the situation is even more precarious for families living in poverty. The family advocate Amada Morales finds

January 2016, https://www.childwelfare.gov/pubPDFs/planning.pdf (accessed July 14, 2019).

118 Legal Information Institute, "Preponderance of Evidence," Cornell Law School, https://www.law.cornell.edu/wex/preponderance_of_the_evidence (accessed September 11, 2021).

119 Tobis, *From Pariahs to Partners*, 153.

the lack of rights afforded parents in CPS cases appalling. She states, "The risk of permanently losing your child is the worst punishment and so should be held to the highest legal standard."[120] Although parents are not guaranteed a lawyer, CAPTA requires that every child be assigned a guardian ad litem when a maltreatment case results in a judicial hearing. Normally, this happens at the first CHIPS hearing. Depending on the state, the guardian ad litem may be a lawyer or a court-appointed special advocate. In either case, the guardian ad litem has been trained to represent the best interests of the child.[121]

As previously stated, a petition to terminate parental rights must be filed when a child has been in out-of-home care for fifteen of the last twenty-two months. There are very few exceptions to this federal statute. Based on her experience with the child welfare system, Roberts asserts the primary reason for parental rights being terminated is that "parents took too long to jump through the hoops." In other words, it has become standard practice for children to be permanently separated from their parents not because the parent had harmed their child or were a danger to them but because they "failed to fulfill some provision on a caseworker's list."[122] Because of the danger imposed by the fifteen-month rule, Amada Morales regularly reminds mothers to mark down the fifteen-month date in their calendars. Much of Morales's work is helping mothers fulfill their conditions in a timely manner. Like Roberts, Morales has frequently witnessed the permanent separation of families based solely on some condition not being completely fulfilled by the fifteen-month mark.[123]

---

120 Amada Morales, interview by author, Milwaukee, WI, August 6, 2018.

121 US Children's Bureau, "Representation of Children in Child Abuse and Neglect Proceedings," Child Welfare Information Gateway, 2021, https://www.childwelfare.gov/pubpdfs/represent.pdf (accessed March 18, 2023).

122 Roberts, *Torn Apart*, 189.

123 Amada Morales, interview by author, Milwaukee, WI, February 6, 2022.

CONCLUSION

Throughout the entire CPS process, parents experience a loss of control. In addition to possibly losing their children, they may be ordered to attend parenting classes and therapy while maintaining stable housing and employment. When children are removed, a host of decisions will be made about their children, usually without the parents' input. Children may be exposed to new cultural and religious traditions without the consent of the parents. All this, along with being scrutinized by CPS workers, can make it very difficult to parent.[124]

The counselor educator Sheri Pickover and the therapist Heather Brown comment on this process as follows:

> The infantilization or role reversal of the birth parents . . . [occurs when] the child welfare system tends to treat birth parents like children and take away their parental and adult authority. This process can be as obvious as not referring to the parents by their last names, referring to them as "the mother" or "the father" rather than by their given names (which sends a message of dismissal—the person only exists in relation to the child), or disregarding their concerns regarding the child.[125]

The guiding mantra throughout the process is always the best interests of the child. The notion of the best interests of the child is employed to justify government intervention in the life of the family. But exactly what is in the best interests of the child is an unsettled issue with assumptions that have changed over time. Until the late nineteenth century,

124 Pickover and Brown, *Therapeutic Interventions*, 41–43.
125 Pickover and Brown, *Therapeutic Interventions*, 42.

children were viewed as property of their father in the United States. The father had ultimate authority in making decisions for his children, and child custody would normally be given to the father during divorce proceedings unless the father wished it otherwise.[126]

Beginning in the late nineteenth century, the tender-years doctrine came into vogue in the United States. This trend followed the opinion of psychology at the time, which believed it was best for children to be nurtured by their mother, who had formed a special bond with each child during infancy. As this belief became more widely accepted, courts began awarding young children to the mother in custody disputes.[127] In modern CPS cases, safety and permanence are the main values utilized in determining the best interests of the child. But the tools used to measure the possibility of future harm are nebulous and vary greatly from state to state. And as the legal process is rarely quick, the law favors finding adoptive parents since the filing of the termination of parental rights petitions is normally required for children who have been out of the home for fifteen of the last twenty-two months.[128]

Coincidentally, the move toward emphasizing the best interests of the child coincided with the disproportionate

126 Mary Ann Mason, *From Father's Property to Children's Rights* (New York: Columbia University Press, 1994), 49–83.

127 June Carbone, "Legal Applications of the 'Best Interest of the Child' Standard," Supplement, *Pediatrics* 134, no. 2 (October 2014): S111–S120, on p. S113, http://pediatrics.aappublications.org/content/pediatrics/134/Supplement_2/S111.full.pdf (accessed September 29, 2018); Ramsay Laing Klaff, "The Tender Years Doctrine: A Defense," *California Law Review* 70, no. 2 (March 1982): 335–72, on pp. 337–48; Mason, *From Father's Property*, 49–83.

128 US Children's Bureau, "Determining the Best Interests of the Child," Child Welfare Information Gateway, 2016, https://www.childwelfare.gov/pubPDFs/best_interest.pdf (accessed September 29, 2018).

increase of Black children in foster care during the 1960s. This also coincided with the move away from foster care being largely voluntary to being involuntarily enforced on families. Roberts notes that one of the Black Codes passed immediately following the Civil War permitted Black children to be "bound out" for work on the plantations of white families. Roberts continues, "These laws gave judges unfettered discretion to place Black children in the care and service of white people if they found the parents to be unfit, unmarried, unemployed and if the they deemed the displacement 'better for the habits and comfort of the child.'"[129] This quote from a Black Code in North Carolina is eerily similar to the logic of the "best interests" of the child. As we will see in the following chapters, once a child is placed in foster care, the "best interests of the child" doctrine allows judges to terminate parental rights based on their perception that Black children will have a better life and be endowed with better habits with a white family in the suburbs.

The permanency aspect of the fifteen out of twenty-two rule concerns the fact that the longer a child is in an out-of-home placement, the more likely another change in placement will occur. Repeated placement changes for children are potentially harmful because they "are associated with an increase in children's externalizing problems and internalizing disorders."[130] In addition to the initial trauma experienced by children taken from their parents, this trauma and its effects only increase with additional out-of-home placements. Additional placements also increase the likelihood that the child will mistrust CPS workers, the foster care system, and foster parents.[131] Oddly, the potential trauma caused children by removing them from their parents is

129 Roberts, *Torn Apart*, 97.
130 Berrick, "Trends and Issues," 26.
131 Pickover and Brown, *Therapeutic Interventions*, 30.

given less weight by almost everyone involved in the child welfare system.

CPS overreach is not only a concern for those passionate about racial justice but also for those on the political right. In a 2017 article in the far-right magazine *The New American*, the political scientist Joe Wolverton expressed trepidation over the fifteen-month rule imposed by ASFA. He believes this policy has led to an "intrusive, invasive, generally unaccountable, and unchallengeable CPS . . . [that] violates the sanctity of the family."[132] Far-right critics of CPS are usually more concerned about parental rights for homeschooling and vaccinations, and this is where white conservative parents are harassed by the same mechanisms that cause pain and trauma to any family unjustly involved with CPS.

If, through this brief history of CPS and the examination of the CPS apparatus, one wanted to give the benefit of the doubt to the policymakers who created this system, one would have to conclude that their good intentions have led to horrible evils. As the Scripture scholar David Frankfurter states, "Historically verifiable atrocities take place not in the ceremonies of some evil realm or as expressions of some ontological evil force, but rather in the course of *purging* evil and its alleged devotees from the world."[133] I believe some of the policies that have led to untold harm were intentional; others were implemented with the best of intentions to root out a real or perceived evil, but the policies were reckless and revealed unacknowledged prejudice toward impoverished whites and African Americans.

Democrats and Republicans often argue over the role and size of federal government. The Republican Party touts

132 Joe Wolverton II, "Help! Government Kidnapped My Child!," *New American*, October 23, 2017, 17–23, on p. 18.

133 David Frankfurter, *Evil Incarnate: Rumors of Demonic Conspiracy and Satanic Abuse in History* (Princeton, NJ: Princeton University Press, 2006), 224.

the need for smaller government but has supported pouring money into CPS while expanding its powers. The Democratic Party has promoted greater government oversight of powerful private institutions and support for civil rights legislation for Black Americans. Nevertheless, it has financed CPS and their many privately funded institutions and endowed them with complete discretion to interfere in the lives of Black families with little accountability. Essentially, there is bipartisan support to keep channeling money into CPS. Neither party wants to be seen as protecting child abusers.

This chapter provided a brief history of CPS and illustrated the basic protocols followed after a complaint is made to CPS. To better understand how this history and these protocols interact with issues of race and class, the following chapter presents a closer look at anti-Black racism and poverty in the United States as well as how these issues have intersected with CPS.

TWO

Under Investigation: Race and Child Welfare

The previous chapter provided a general history of CPS in the United States that will be crucial in moving forward. It is much easier to propose a path forward after we know how we arrived in our current situation. The purpose of this chapter is to thoroughly analyze the relationship between anti-Black racism and CPS. We begin by looking generally at racism in the United States and how the War on Drugs contributed to the problem of racial disproportionality in the child welfare system. We then survey the intersection of anti-Black racism and CPS in the twenty-first century. This will include sharing the story of a CPS visitation provider turned activist and an evaluation of out-of-home placement practices, the role of poverty, and the acceptability of unjust practices toward investigated families. We close with reviewing the role of medical institutions in harming Black families and how the Americans with Disabilities Act helped one family whose parental rights had been terminated. Real-life stories of investigated families are interspersed throughout the chapter.

RACISM IN AMERICA

Racism is so detrimental to African Americans that it also affects their health. For example, even though the United

States ranks first in per capita healthcare spending, it ranks 55th out of 225 countries in rates for infant mortality. And infant mortality rates for Black infants are almost twice as high as the national average. After birth defects, low birth weight is the leading cause of infant mortality. Low birth weights are twice as likely among Black infants compared to white infants. Recent research indicates that the racism faced by Black mothers in the United States is a significant factor in producing chronic stress, a cause of low birth weight. The racial disparity in low birth weights remains unchanged even when income, prenatal care, and education are taken into account. Researchers have even discovered that the likelihood of an infant with a low birth weight increases for Black African immigrants to the United States the longer they live here.[1]

The danger faced by African Americans in deadly confrontations with the police—with some horrific instances being captured on film—has received media attention this past decade. Referring to the lynchings and killings of African Americans by police, the Christian ethicist Elias Ortega-Aponte states, "An all-too-common occurrence yesterday and today, part of the everydayness of living while Black, the possibility of joy is always threatened. A Black body, man, woman, or child, subjected to abuse—far too often, abuse unto death."[2] Ortega-Aponte continues, "As it pertains to Black lives, our country lacks love for justice, and perhaps even a concept of it."[3]

1 Esther Gross, Victoria Efetevbia, and Alexandria Wilkins, "Racism and Sexism against Black Women May Contribute to High Rates of Black Infant Mortality," *Child Trends*, April 18, 2019, https://www.childtrends.org/racism-sexism-against-black-women-may-contribute-high-rates-black-infant-mortality (accessed April 19, 2019).

2 Elias Ortega-Aponte, "The Haunting of Lynching Spectacles," in *Anti-Blackness and Christian Ethics*, ed. Vincent W. Lloyd and Andrew Prevot (Maryknoll, NY: Orbis Books, 2017), 111–28, on p. 116.

3 Ortega-Aponte, "Haunting of Lynching Spectacles," 122.

Although the focus of this book is not on CPS caseworkers, most are grossly unprepared and undertrained. Fewer than 40 percent of CPS workers have a degree in social work.[4] The sociologist Richard Gelles observes that though most have college degrees, it is very common for CPS agencies to "offer no more than twenty hours of training before a new worker assumes a full caseload."[5] In addition, 67 percent of welfare workers are white, with only 19.5 percent of workers being Black.[6] Just as there is a pattern of white police officers "fearing for their lives" without justification when confronting a Black body, there is also a pattern of white social workers fearing for the lives of children in the care of a Black parent without justification. In the former case, a Black man may be unjustly killed by the police; in the latter case, a Black mother may unjustly have her children removed and her parental rights terminated.

Racism is not limited to one aspect of US society but permeates every part of it. Bryan Massingale asserts that racialized sexual stereotypes "are used as a pretext or justification for social exclusion, inequality, subjugation, control, denigration, and inferiority." For example, he sees the stereotype of Black women as sexually promiscuous used as justification for harsh welfare policies.[7] Kelly Brown Douglas asserts that the hypersexualizing of Black bodies was originally done "to support the sexual abuse of the Black body during slavery."[8] Ibram Kendi also links the popular stories of "aggressive hypersexual African femininity" in the colonial

4 Richard P. Barth et al., "Child Welfare Worker Characteristics and Job Satisfaction: A National Study," *Social Work* 53, no. 3 (July 2008): 199–209, on p. 203.

5 Gelles, *Out of Harm's Way*, 3.

6 Barth et al., "Child Welfare Worker," 203–4.

7 Bryan N. Massingale, "The Erotic Life of Anti-Blackness," in *Anti-Blackness and Christian Ethics*, ed. Vincent W. Lloyd and Andrew Prevot (Maryknoll, NY: Orbis Books, 2017), 173–94, on pp. 175–76.

8 Douglas, *Stand Your Ground*, 65.

period with exonerating "White men of their inhuman rapes and to mask their human attractions to the supposed beast-like women."[9]

Douglas believes that past and present "white culture in all of its expressions is intrinsically violent, given its necessary anti-Black nature . . . anti-Black violence is a part of America's original DNA."[10] Recognizing separate narratives for white and Black women in the United States, she states, "While white women were considered virginal, pure angels in need of protection, Black women were considered wanton, lascivious Jezebels in need of controlling."[11] Douglas asserts that although the US narrative views a Black man as predatory, a Black woman "is often portrayed as criminally immoral and most times mean and angry."[12]

In another work, Douglas further explains, "This portrayal of Black women as angry is the female version of the dangerous Black man."[13] If a Black woman, even unconsciously, is seen as a criminal, angry, and in need of being controlled, the CPS system will believe itself justified in removing her children. As Douglas avers, Black mothers are seen "as responsible for raising the 'criminalblackman.'"[14] If one believes the myth that Black women raise criminals, then placing those children with white suburban parents is the appropriate—though twisted—response to that myth.

---

9 Kendi, *Stamped from the Beginning*, 41–42.

10 Kelly Brown Douglas, "More than Skin Deep," in *Anti-Blackness and Christian Ethics*, ed. Vincent W. Lloyd and Andrew Prevot (Maryknoll, NY: Orbis Books, 2017), 3–18, on p. 9.

11 Douglas, "More than Skin Deep," 12. For more on the Jezebel stereotype, see Lee, *Black Madonna*, 16–18.

12 Douglas, "More than Skin Deep," 14. For more on the angry Black woman stereotype, see Lee, *Black Madonna*, 19–20.

13 Douglas, *Stand Your Ground*, 85.

14 Douglas, *Stand Your Ground*, 84.

A brief analysis of the term *pickaninny* may shed further light on the history of racism faced by the African American family in the United States. *Pickaninny* is a racial slur for a child of African descent, particularly those with darker skin. A simple Google image search will result in a plethora of offensive images. The US historian Robin Bernstein importantly perceives, "Pickaninnies [Black children] often wear ragged clothes (which suggest parental neglect) and are sometimes partially or fully naked."[15] Within the wheelhouse of American bigotry, it is a long-held stereotype that African American parents are unable to properly care for their children. When combined with the stereotype of the angry Black woman, we can begin to understand the precarious situation of Black families accosted by a CPS worker.

Repeated studies have revealed the implicit bias of white Americans toward Black Americans, even when white people desire to view all races fairly. A video game study presented participants with pictures of Black and white subjects, some holding guns and some holding benign objects. The participant had to quickly decide whether to shoot or not. Unsurprisingly, they were more likely to shoot unarmed Black people and refrain from shooting armed white people. Studies also show that jurors and law enforcement become more punitive with criminal suspects as their skin color becomes darker and more lenient as their skin color becomes lighter.[16]

15 Robin Bernstein, *Racial Innocence: Performing American Childhood from Slavery to Civil Rights* (New York University Press, 2011), 34.

16 Alexander, *New Jim Crow*, 106–7; Joshua Correll et al., "The Police Officer's Dilemma: Using Ethnicity to Disambiguate Potentially Threatening Individuals," *Journal of Personality and Social Psychology* 83 (December 2002), 1314; Jennifer L. Eberhardt et al., "Looking Deathworthy," *Psychological Science* 17, no. 5 (2006): 383–86; Jennifer L. Eberhardt et al., "Seeing Black: Race, Crime, and Visual Processing," *Journal of Personality and Social Psychology* 87, no. 6 (2004): 876–93.

Although poverty plays a role in the injustices faced by African Americans, class alone cannot account for the entire situation. The African American experience of chattel slavery continues to leave an indelible mark on how the Black person is viewed in the United States. As the Black Catholic theologian M. Shawn Copeland writes, "Chattel slavery relegated a human living person to be used or discarded at the whim of the owner."[17] Over nearly 250 years, more than three hundred thousand Black Africans were transported to English America (and later the United States). Slavery officially ended with the passage of the Thirteenth Amendment in 1865. But for the nearly 100 years that followed, Jim Crow, segregation, and lynching were common practices across the United States. Since the passage of the Civil Rights Act of 1964, anti-Black racism has simply changed form once again.

Racial discrimination still exists in housing, medicine, employment, education, policing, Child Protective Services, and so on. As the historian Ibram Kendi recognizes, the Civil Rights Act of 1964 "legislated against clear and obvious 'intention to discriminate.'" Kendi further explains, "If the northern backers of the act defined policies as racist by their public outcomes instead of their public intent . . . discriminators had to merely privatize their public policies to get around the Civil Rights Act."[18] In other words, unless a person or group is open in stating its policy meant to discriminate against African Americans, it will be nearly impossible for courts to see such actions as violating the Civil Rights Act. For example, the statistically disproportionate removal of Black children or the disproportionate jailing of African Americans does not violate the Civil Rights Act unless intent to discriminate can be uncovered.

17 M. Shawn Copeland, *Knowing Christ Crucified* (Maryknoll, NY: Orbis Books, 2018), 13–14.

18 Kendi, *Stamped from the Beginning*, 386.

Michelle Alexander has detected this same problem in how the Supreme Court interprets the Fourteenth Amendment, which guarantees equal protection under the law regardless of race. She points to the 1987 case *McCleskey v. Kemp*, in which a Black man faced the death penalty for killing a white police officer in Georgia. The defense brought forth strong evidence illustrating that the death penalty was sought for Black defendants with white victims 70 percent of the time but for white defendants with Black victims only 19 percent of the time. Alexander states, "The Court rejected McCleskey's claims under the Fourteenth Amendment, insisting that unless McCleskey could prove that the prosecutor in his particular case had sought the death penalty because of race or that the jury had imposed it for racial reasons, the statistical evidence . . . did not prove unequal treatment under the law."[19]

In the majority opinion for the case, the court stated, "If we accepted McCleskey's claim that racial bias has impermissibly tainted the capital sentencing decision, we could soon be faced with similar claims as to other types of penalty."[20] Essentially, the Supreme Court was worried that observable patterns of racism would require undesirable changes in the criminal justice system to make it racially just. This same attitude is present with CPS policymakers and has allowed the inequalities present in CPS to exist for decades. It is a blatant denial of the prevailing racist conditions that plague US society.

CPS AND THE WAR ON DRUGS

Researchers have struggled to pinpoint the source of this disproportionality in CPS. They readily admit the problem is

19 Alexander, *New Jim Crow*, 109–11.

20 *McCleskey v Kemp*, quoted in Alexander, *New Jim Crow*, 111.

compounded by the fact that there is no way to measure the actual number of child maltreatment cases in the United States by race.[21] Nevertheless, the issue of disproportionality continues.

The previous chapter linked the War on Drugs to the increase in racial disparity that occurred with CPS during the 1980s. The effects of the War on Drugs on racial disparity within CPS still reverberate today. As the American Civil Liberties Union (ACLU) reported in 2013, during the first decade of the twenty-first century, there were over eight million marijuana arrests, with someone being arrested every thirty-seven seconds. Arrest rates for African Americans were 3.73 times higher than those for whites despite no statistical difference in the percentage of Black and white Americans using marijuana.[22] In 2020, the second leading cause of removal was drug abuse by the parent, resulting in 35 percent of removals. (It should also be noted that more than one reason can be listed for removal, so there is some overlap in these percentages.)[23]

The degree of evidence needed to list drug use on a parent's file varies widely from state to state. Some states require a formal diagnosis of chemical dependency for it to be listed as the official reason. Others only require a positive urine

21 John Fluke, PhD, Brenda Jones Harden, PhD, Molly Jenkins, MSW, Ashleigh Ruehrdanz, and American Human Association, "A Research Synthesis on Child Welfare Disproportionality and Disparities," (papers from a research symposium convened by the Center for the Study of Social Policy and the Annie E. Casey Foundation on behalf of the Alliance for Racial Equity in Child Welfare), 1–93, on pp. 64–65, https://www.aecf.org/resources/disparities-and-disproportionality-in-child-welfare (accessed December 14, 2021).

22 American Civil Liberties Union, "The War on Marijuana in Black and White," June 2013, https://www.aclu.org/report/report-war-marijuana-black-and-white?redirect=criminal-law-reform/war-marijuana-black-and-white (accessed July 14, 2019).

23 Children's Bureau, *The AFCARS Report*, no. 28, 2.

test or the suspicion of the CPS worker. Furthermore, many removals that are connected to drug use may simply be designated as cases of neglect, which is the most common reason for removals, at 64 percent.[24]

Our main concern is that the disproportionate number of arrests for African Americans using drugs can also lead to increased scrutiny by CPS. About forty-seven states currently have child welfare laws that pertain to illegal drug use by the parent.[25] Evidence indicates that within the CPS system, African American parents are more likely to be referred to drug treatment but are less likely to attend treatment. White families had the highest participation rate. The reason for this is attributed to the relative inaccessibility of drug treatment services in many African American neighborhoods and greater accessibility of these services for white families.[26]

CPS AND BLACK FAMILIES IN THE TWENTY-FIRST CENTURY

Dorothy Roberts laments that despite the disproportionate harm to Black families, "most contemporary critiques of the child welfare system barely acknowledge the importance

24 Kristin Sepulveda and Sarah Catherine Williams, "One in Three Children Entered Foster Care in 2017 Because of Parental Drug Abuse," *Child Trends*, February 26, 2019, https://www.childtrends.org/one-in-three-children-entered-foster-care-in-fy-2017-because-of-parental-drug-abuse (accessed July 14, 2019); Children's Bureau, *The AFCARS Report*, no. 28, 2.

25 Children's Bureau, "Parental Substance Use and the Child Welfare System," Project Lifeline, October 2014, 4–5, https://projectlifeline.us/wp-content/uploads/2020/09/Child-Welfare-System.pdf (accessed March 8, 2023).

26 Children's Bureau, "Racial Disproportionality and Disparity in Child Welfare," November 2016, 10, https://www.childwelfare.gov/pubpdfs/racial_disproportionality.pdf (accessed July 14, 2019).

of race. . . . Their primary goal is to make services more sensitive to the needs and culture of Black families, not to question the fundamental conflict between the child welfare system and the integrity of the Black family and community."[27] She refers to CPS as "a state-run program that disrupts, restructures, and polices Black families."[28]

In early 2017, a federal civil rights lawsuit was filed against the Texas governor Greg Abbott and Henry Whitman Jr., commissioner of the Texas Department of Family and Protective Services because of the treatment faced by Black families in Texas. Similar to national numbers, Black children are four times as likely to be placed in foster care as white and Hispanic children.[29] This issue brought together several anti-racism groups in Texas, including Black Administrators in Child Welfare, the National Association of Blacks in Social Work, and Black Lives Matter.[30] Unfortunately, the suit was dismissed, with the judge stating that federal courts lacked jurisdiction. The appealing of state judgments on the grounds of a civil rights or a constitutional matter can only be reviewed on the federal level by the Supreme Court.[31]

Amada Morales declares that when a Black child is removed from their urban family and placed with a suburban white family, the child is cut off not only from their

27 Roberts, *Shattered Bonds*, vii.

28 Roberts, *Shattered Bonds*, viii.

29 Gabrielle Banks, "Federal Lawsuit Accuses Texas, CPS of Discriminating against Black Children," *Houston Chronicle*, May 24, 2017, http://www.chron.com/news/houston-texas/article/Caretaker-aunt-says-CPS-put-nephew-up-for-11167022.php.

30 Banks, "Federal Lawsuit Accuses Texas."

31 A summary of the judgment with its reasoning can be found in "Maravi Moore v. Hank Whitman, et al.," *Justia US Law*, https://law.justia.com/cases/federal/appellate-courts/ca5/18-20069/18-20069-2018-07-26.html (accessed December 30, 2021).

biological parents but also their extended family, school, community, and culture.[32] Roberts expresses a similar sentiment: "Parents' freedom to raise their children is important not only to individuals but also to the welfare or even survival of ethnic, cultural, and religious groups. Weakening the parent-child bond and disintegrating families within a group are a means of subordinating the entire group."[33] The counselor educator Sheri Pickover and the therapist Heather Brown explain some of the basic trauma a child experiences when removed from the home: "Children in foster care do not only lose a parent or parents when they are removed from their homes; they lose their homes, their bedrooms, their neighborhoods, their siblings, their extended relatives, their toys and other belongings, their school connections, and their peers and friends. These losses are compounded and overwhelming, especially for a child. Expect children to experience an adjustment disorder and signs of grief and/or complicated grief for several months following the removal."[34]

Pickover and Brown explain that when removal is necessary, it is best to place the child in a similar cultural, ethnic, racial, and religious setting.[35] They state that differences in these background characteristics "can cause identity concerns for the child as well as exacerbate other presenting concerns."[36] An additional obstacle facing parents whose children have been placed with prospective adopters with greater financial resources than the biological parents is that many courts decide it is in the best interests of the child to be

32 Amada Morales, "The Effects of Privatizing Social Service Programs on Black Children and Families" (presented at United Nations Association of Greater Milwaukee, Milwaukee, WI, March 10, 2018).

33 Roberts, *Shattered Bonds*, 233.

34 Pickover and Brown, *Therapeutic Interventions*, 26.

35 Pickover and Brown, *Therapeutic Interventions*, 82.

36 Pickover and Brown, *Therapeutic Interventions*, 82.

with the prospective adopters because of the increased access to resources. It is in these tragic situations that one can see the result of the 1990s legislation that limited welfare benefits while permitting transracial adoption.

The psychological effects on children from being separated from their birth parents are also troubling. A child's grief over removal can last several months, with ensuing complications that can have a lasting impact for years. The trauma experienced can result in the child acting out, including difficulty sleeping, nightmares, eating issues, anger issues, and acting out physically and sexually. Older children may miss school, run away, or try to return to their parents. Part of this acting out may be done with the hope that it will result in their being returned home.[37]

AMADA MORALES'S JOURNEY FROM CPS WORKER TO FAMILY ADVOCATE

From 2009 to 2012, Amada Morales was a visitation provider for a private corporation in Milwaukee that was subcontracted to supervise family visits. Morales was paid twenty dollars per hour for supervising family visits. The federal government provides sixty dollars per hour per child for supervised family visits. Subcontracted agencies in Wisconsin receive anywhere from forty to sixty dollars per hour per child depending on their contract.[38] Morales remembers feeling "most guilty for being paid $20 an hour to take a gorgeous, six-month-old brown baby to visit her birth mother. The mom was young, a mother of seven. I was specifically asked to document if I noticed roaches." After the visit, she drove the baby back to the "beautiful, ranch-style home in a suburb, where she was wanted by two very clean, white, tidy,

37 Pickover and Brown, *Therapeutic Interventions*, 26–27.

38 Amada Morales, interview by author, Milwaukee, WI, March 26, 2020.

nurturing lesbian women. I know they didn't love the little girl more than the birth mom." The CPS professionals she knew reminded her that the adoption would give the girl "a better life." In the end, "the mother was torn from her seven children because, as I witnessed, the couple wanted to hurry and adopt the baby."[39]

The privatized CPS agency negotiated an agreement with the couple to also adopt two of the baby's siblings, even though they only wanted the baby girl. Morales concludes, "Just business as usual. Money is exchanged for these children, and everyone is getting paid except the parents who created the children. These children are being trafficked by the state like slaves were torn from their mothers—separated forever without a trace."[40] In this case, three of the seven kids were eventually returned to the mother. This begs the question: If the mother was so dangerous, why was it safe to leave any children with her? Morales believes it was less about the condition of the mother and more about filling a need of privileged whites to adopt children. As Morales explains, "I was being paid to help richer, privileged people tear a poor, young Black woman from her infant and other children."[41] In the case just noted by Morales, the mother had a low IQ. This is supposed to create a special circumstance under the Americans with Disabilities Act that will be covered later.

Another issue Morales confronted during her time as a visitation provider was that there was an incentive against terminating supervised visits to progress to unsupervised visits. If supervised visits go well, the parents are supposed to "graduate" to unsupervised visits with their children.

39 Amada Morales, *Child Welfare Trafficking of Children in Poverty* (Milwaukee, WI: Welfare Warriors, 2020). Amada Morales, interview by author, March 10, 2020.

40 Morales, *Child Welfare Trafficking.*

41 Morales, *Child Welfare Trafficking.*

Unsupervised visits are seen by the presiding judge as a necessary step toward reunification. Amada Morales, her coworkers, and her company were only paid for supervised visits. Unsupervised visits do not benefit the subcontractor or its employees.[42]

Morales shared that the problem was not her private contractor employer. She was never pressured to prevent a family from graduating from unsupervised to supervised visits. Though she could not be sure, Morales assumed her managers were not concerned about unsupervised visits because there were so many cases for the company that the business was not harmed by a few graduations. But for her fellow workers, allowing good parents to graduate to unsupervised visits could affect their take-home pay if there was not another family for whom they could conduct supervised visits. For unsupervised visits, workers were only paid for dropping off and picking up the kids; they would not get paid while parents visited their kids.

The primary reason given by her coworkers for not graduating a family was that the parents' home had not been checked for safety, but the parents have no control over this. Morales also witnessed her coworkers make false statements, such as stating that a mother did not know how to discipline her kids, the kids were having a hard time adjusting after visits, or a mother did not bring food.[43]

Seeing mother after mother being denied the opportunity of unsupervised visits as her coworkers reaped financial rewards left a bad taste in Amada Morales's mouth. She began to examine the child welfare system more deeply and discovered a confounding system that was overflowing with

42 Morales, interview, March 26, 2020. For more information about parents with a learning disability and CPS, see Penny Morgan, *Child Protection and Parents with a Learning Disability: Good Practice for Assessing and Working with Adults* (London: Jessica Kingsley Publishers, 2017).

43 Morales, interview, March 26, 2020.

mechanisms to prevent good parents from reuniting with their children. Morales explains, "My conscience drove me to get advice from a famous activist leader at the Welfare Warriors."[44]

When Morales was a young child, her mother volunteered with the Welfare Warriors. Sometimes, her mother would bring Amada with her. At the moment when Morales was struggling with the morality of well-paid work, she remembered her mother's involvement with these activists, who organized mothers to fight for their families. Shortly afterward, Morales became a nonpaid family court advocate and activist and has now dedicated years of her life to preserving families.[45]

OUT-OF-HOME PLACEMENT

Every time there is the rare and tragic occurrence of a child who dies because of maltreatment by a parent after CPS determined it was safe to keep the child at home, the pressure increases for CPS investigators to err on the side of removing children from their homes. From 2011 to 2020, an average of about three children died in Wisconsin while they had an open CPS case; 2011 saw the highest number of incidences with nine deaths, and 2015 saw the lowest with zero.[46] Although preventing the death of a child must be a priority, it is unjust and harmful to families to remove thousands of children who could stay home with their primary caretaker without any concern for how the removal will affect the rest of the child's life.

In 2017 in Wisconsin, 36.9 percent of the 3,332 white child victims were placed in out-of-home care, and 48.5 percent

44 Morales, *Child Welfare Trafficking*.
45 Morales, interview, March 26, 2020.
46 Wisconsin Reports.

of the 1,247 Black child victims were placed in out-of-home care.[47] That means that Black child victims were removed from the home 31 percent more often than white child victims. The situation becomes more complicated when we add the number of children removed from the home without a substantiated case of child maltreatment. In 2017, 809 white children were placed in out-of-home care without an allegation, compared to 623 Black children.[48] To be clear, more Black children were placed in out-of-home care without a substantiated allegation of maltreatment than those who had one.

For both white and Black children, the overwhelming reason for removal of a child who was not determined to be a victim in Wisconsin was neglect or caretaker challenge. *Caretaker challenge* indicates the belief that the parent is unable to properly care for their children, with the most common examples being lack of adequate housing and substance abuse.[49] A case of substantiated maltreatment requires there be a substantiated perpetrator of maltreatment. When a child is determined to not be a victim, it is because the CPS investigator did not believe either there was a preponderance of evidence that child maltreatment had occurred or there was a preponderance of evidence that indicated an individual—such as a parent—was the source of any perceived maltreatment.

To present the statistics in another way, 39.7 percent of white children placed in out-of-home care did not have a substantiated allegation of maltreatment, while 50.7 percent of Black children placed in out-of-home care were placed

47 Wisconsin Report 2017.

48 This information is not included in the State of Wisconsin reports for CPS. This information was obtained directly through the Wisconsin Department of Children and Families (WIDCF) via email. In future footnotes, I'll refer to data obtained in this manner as "Provided in WIDCF correspondence."

49 Provided in WIDCF correspondence.

without a substantiated allegation of maltreatment.[50] Furthermore, the number of children being removed without a substantiated allegation has been slowly increasing in Wisconsin. In 2011, 535 white children were removed without a substantiated allegation. In 2018, the number of white children in this category increased to 826. For Black children, the increase has been slower, with 486 Black children removed without a substantiated allegation of maltreatment in 2011 compared to 544 in 2018.[51]

There has been more of an effort in recent years to prioritize out-of-home placements with a relative, which is known as kinship care. Kinship care is normally viewed in a positive light because of its ability to lessen the emotional trauma on children by keeping them with a known family member. Nevertheless, Marian S. Harris and Ada Skyles have noted that African American children are disproportionately placed in kinship care to their own disadvantage. They state, "Difficult caseloads and the willingness of African American families to assume responsibility for kin may encourage child welfare practitioners to overlook the needs of birth parents when African American children are placed in kinship care and thus may reduce the likelihood of reunification."[52]

This is indeed the case. Fewer children in kinship care are reunified with their parents, especially African American children.[53] This is particularly disconcerting since children reunified after kinship care are less likely to reenter the CPS system.[54] Though exact figures are difficult to determine, an estimated 20–40 percent of children who are reunified with their parents will reenter the foster care system at some point

50 Provided in WIDCF correspondence.

51 Provided in WIDCF correspondence.

52 Harris and Skyles, "Kinship Care," 34–35; A similar argument is made by Berrick, "Trends and Issues," 29–31.

53 Harris and Skyles, "Kinship Care," 40.

54 Harris and Skyles, "Kinship Care," 36.

during the following five years.[55] One statistic many studies agree on is that children are significantly less likely to reenter foster care if their original foster care placement was with relatives as compared to strangers.[56]

Grandmothers and Kinship Care in Wisconsin

When children are placed in out-of-home care, the stated goal of the Wisconsin model is to transition children "safely and quickly back with their family, whenever possible, or to another permanent home."[57] This means the primary goal regarding children in foster care is for them to be quickly—and safely—reunited with their family. If this is not possible, the state wants to find another stable setting for the children. Unfortunately, this is often not the case, not even when grandmothers are involved. To celebrate International Women's Day in March 2020, the Welfare Warriors organized a celebration at the University of Wisconsin-Milwaukee, where they presented awards to five Black grandmothers in the Milwaukee area who have fought tirelessly to keep their grandchildren in the family.

In each case, a grandchild had been removed and placed with white foster parents outside the City of Milwaukee—in one case, the children were placed outside the State of Wisconsin. These grandmothers, with their strong sense of family and familial obligation, labored to either have their

55 Sarah Font, Kierra Sattler, and Elizabeth Gershoff, "When Home Is Still Unsafe: From Family Reunification to Foster Care Reentry," *Journal of Marriage and Family* 80, no. 5 (October 2018): 1333–43, https://www.ncbi.nlm.nih.gov/pmc/articles/PMC6251317/ (accessed July 3, 2020).

56 Barth et al., "Reentry of Elementary-Aged Children Following Reunification from Foster Care" *Children and Youth Services Review* 30, no. 4 (April 2008): 353–64, https://www.ncbi.nlm.nih.gov/pmc/articles/PMC3134969/ (accessed March 8, 2023); Font et al., "When Home Is Still Unsafe."

57 Wisconsin Report 2015, 1.2.

grandchildren returned to their sons and daughters or—at a minimum—have their grandchildren placed in grandma's custody. Each grandmother shared her story during the awards ceremony. It was heartbreaking. Some cried tears of joy because they had succeeded in reunifying their family, while others shed tears of sorrow because the familial connection to their grandchildren had been terminated by the courts.[58]

Nettie was one of the grandmothers successful in helping her son be reunified with his three children. Her son Jon was in prison for ten months on a drug offense. Jon's children had been removed from the custody of his former girlfriend and co-parent due to neglect. The children's mother was suffering from a terrible drug addiction and was soon living on the streets. The mother was found murdered in her car not long afterward. Jon wanted to get his kids back, but he could not meet any of his conditions while serving his prison term. When the children were originally removed, Nettie had filed for a guardianship request, but the CPS worker had denied her request and placed the three young children with a white couple in Sheboygan (an hour north of Milwaukee) who wanted to adopt the children.[59]

When Nettie had made her original guardianship petition, the worker told her she was denied placement because she only had a one-bedroom apartment. With Jon in prison and their mom dead, this case quickly became a termination-of-parental-rights (TPR) case. Amada Morales and Patricia McManus, who had been providing support for Nettie, believed the case was lost based on how TPR cases normally

58 My personal notes from being in attendance at International Women's Day Celebration, sponsored by the Welfare Warriors at University of Wisconsin-Milwaukee, March 8, 2020, hereafter referred to as International Women's Day notes.

59 International Women's Day notes; Morales, interview by author, November 29, 2021.

go when parents are in prison. But Nettie did not give up. After having her guardianship petition denied, she had commandeered a three-bedroom apartment and reapplied for guardianship. The judge wanted to seriously consider this petition, which slowed down the TPR process. It was at this point that the judge discovered the worker had originally decided to deny placement to Nettie. Since family members are supposed to have priority in a child placement, this did not please the judge.[60]

At this point, Jon was released from prison and hit the ground running. Jon loves his children and made sure he met all the conditions set by the judge to be reunited with them. Nevertheless, meeting one's conditions does not guarantee reunification, and CPS still wanted to continue the TPR. But as it became clear the judge was impressed with Jon's effort to improve his situation and be a wonderful father to this children, CPS withdrew its TPR petition. Jon was finally reunified with his three young children after three long years. Jon and his children live with Nettie, who is so happy to have her son and grandchildren all under the same roof. Thinking of this case brings a smile to Amada's face. During the three-year process, the Sheboygan couple had been aggressively trying to adopt the three children. But as Morales states, "Nettie was relentless and persistent." Nettie and Jon succeeded against what seemed to be impossible odds.[61]

There was another African American grandmother, whom I will call Grace. Since CPS workers are supposed to make an effort to place children who are being removed from their home with relatives, CPS contacted Grace to see if she could take her daughter's two young children immediately.

60 International Women's Day notes; Morales, interview, November 29, 2021.

61 International Women's Day notes; Morales, interview, November 29, 2021.

Grace responded that she would be happy to take them in but was wondering if the transfer could be delayed until after her foot surgery the following week or if she could have some help watching her grandchildren for the first few days after her foot surgery. This was not satisfactory to the CPS worker, who denied her access to child care and quickly placed the children with a middle-class white family in the suburbs who was interested in adopting them.[62]

Grace was disappointed that she was denied custody of her grandchildren but scheduled monthly visits with them. When the children arrived, they were filthy, smelled bad, and their hair was matting. Grandma Grace would spend half her time cleaning the kids, giving them decent clothes to wear, and cutting their hair. Every time she saw the children, it was the same story. When Grace asked what happened to the nice clothes she had given her grandchildren, she discovered the foster parents were throwing them in the garbage. In what can only be attributed to spite on the part of the foster parents, they even persuaded the judge to order Grace to stop cutting the children's hair.[63]

The judge did make one right decision in this case: allowing Grace to see her grandkids. The CPS agency and the prospective adopters argued against it, but the judge thought it was good for the children to have a familiar connection. Grace also requested guardianship of the children. If granted, she would have been given custody of her grandkids and become their permanent placement. The custody aspect of guardianship permits the guardian to make medical decisions. The difference between guardianship and adoption is that with guardianship, the parent's rights are not terminated.[64]

62 International Women's Day notes.

63 International Women's Day notes; Morales, interview by author, April 21, 2020.

64 Morales, interview by author, April 30, 2020.

Unfortunately, Grace's story does not have a happy ending. About two months after the International Women's Day celebration, Grace was denied guardianship, and her son's parental rights were terminated. The TPR not only ended the children's relationship with their father but also with Grace and all the family they had ever known before CPS workers removed them from their home. Similar to Nettie's story, Grace's son was also serving a prison sentence. The difference in their two cases was twofold: (1) this time, the father was serving ten years in jail instead of ten months, and (2) Grace had a different judge who was less sympathetic to keeping the children with family members.[65]

If Grace had known how arbitrary some CPS workers can be, she would obviously have just agreed to taking her grandchildren without asking for any help, and this story would most likely have ended with the children staying with their family. The father in this case is appealing the TPR ruling, just as almost every parent Amada Morales works with appeals a TPR ruling. The process takes about two years, but Amada has never seen any of the parents she works with win one of these appeals. It is after the almost-assured appeal failure that the foster parents return to children's court to finalize the legal adoption of the children.[66]

Grace's situation boggles the mind. Here is a loving grandmother who wants to take care of her grandchildren. It is hard to discern why the CPS worker did not accommodate Grace's foot surgery so that her grandchildren could avoid the trauma of being separated from their family and being placed in an alien and neglectful environment. If we assume the CPS worker was not vindictive but simply overworked, the probable reason for this action is that it is much easier

65 International Women's Day notes; Morales, interview, November 29, 2021.

66 International Women's Day notes; Morales, interview, November 29, 2021.

to place the kids with strangers in foster care than to fill out the paperwork to offer child care. Another option was to place Grace's grandchildren in foster care for three weeks while Grace was recovering from surgery. But ASFA favors limiting the number of child placements.

Therefore, placing the children in foster care for three weeks would have looked bad on the reports for the private agency handling the case. The judge assigned to the case could have chosen to place the children with their grandma, but judges normally give the agency discretion with placement and rarely overrule a placement decision made by a CPS agency. Grace could have filed a change-of-placement motion in court in hopes that the judge would overrule the agency's decision, but it often takes months for a judge to decide on such a motion, and the biological family usually loses because of the judge's unwillingness to overrule an agency placement decision.[67]

CAUSES OF RACIAL DISPROPORTIONALITY IN CPS

Dorothy Roberts concludes that no single cause has resulted in a racist CPS institution. Contributing factors include poverty, mandated reporters, caseworker prejudices and misconceptions, and inadequate laws and practices. Additionally, there is "the interplay of societal, structural, and individual factors that feed into each other to determine which families fall under state scrutiny and supervision."[68] Roberts concludes, "Racial bias [is] at every stage of the child protective process."[69]

Unfortunately, there are CPS scholars who do not take seriously the issue of racial disproportionality. With these scholars, there is often a correlation between overemphasizing

67 Morales, interview, April 21, 2020.

68 Roberts, *Shattered Bonds*, 96–97.

69 Roberts, *Shattered Bonds*, 52.

the need to remove children and not viewing racial discrimination as a significant factor in the child welfare system. One of the more prominent examples is the sociologist Richard Gelles, who has been writing on the topic since the 1970s and avers that it is worth wrongly removing some children from their homes in the battle to protect children. In 2017, he published a 186-page book on CPS that dedicates only two full pages to racial disproportionality.[70]

THE ROLE OF POVERTY

Without downplaying the role of anti-Blackness in the CPS system, poverty and class also increase contact with CPS. Lash argues that the child welfare system provides a panacea for US society, which is ravaged by poverty. More than 20 percent of children in the United States live in poverty, which is the highest rate of any developed country. Lash states, "The child welfare system helps to make the impoverishment and social neglect of children tolerable to the larger population by promoting the idea that children are valued and protected. Perhaps of even greater importance, the system situates blame for the danger and harm imposed on children on their families rather than on the material conditions of their existence."[71]

Lash portrays a harsh reality: "Confronted with a child in jeopardy, or a child who has experienced abuse or abandonment, workers must respond to immediate threats, even

70 Gelles, *Out of Harm's Way*, 85–87.

71 Lash, *"When the Welfare People Come,"* 9. In 2012, UNICEF measured child poverty in the thirty-five richest countries of the world. The United States has 23.1 percent of its children living in poverty, ranking next to last, with only Romania having a greater percentage of children living in childhood poverty. UNICEF, *Measuring Child Poverty*, May 2012, 3, https://www.unicef-irc.org/publications/pdf/rc10_eng.pdf (accessed March 7, 2018).

if the underlying, overriding threat is capitalism itself."[72] Essentially, a society that trusts the invisible hand of the market to provide an opportunity for everyone contributes to a child welfare mentality that blames the parents for neglect caused by poverty.

The poverty crisis in the United States does not affect all equally and disproportionately harms African American families. Although 23.1 percent of all children in the United States live in poverty, Black children are three times as likely to live in poverty compared with white children (33 percent and 11 percent, respectively).[73]

The historian Catherine E. Rymph perceives the current CPS system as rooted in "the larger problems with the mid-century American foster care system . . . from the failure of the welfare state to offer true family security, the inherent problems of private/public welfare provision, and the persistent undervaluing of care work."[74] Rymph rightly judges the past and current CPS system as a "poverty program" for funneling impoverished children out of destitute households. Ideally, Americans would provide appropriate family support that would make the use of foster care rare. And under rare circumstances, well-trained foster parents would be available to help when families were facing problems "more complex than those of mere poverty."[75]

Poverty also triggers additional problems that further complicate a family's life. Poverty has been linked to depression in adults. In fact, it "is one of the most significant social

72 Lash, *"When the Welfare People Come,"* 9.

73 This information is from the Annie E. Casey Foundation's Kids Count Data Center, https://datacenter.kidscount.org/data/tables/44-children-in-poverty-by-race-and-ethnicity#detailed/1/any/false/871,870,573,869,36,868,867,133,38,35/10,11,9,12,1,185,13/324,323 (accessed August 6, 2019).

74 Rymph, *Raising Government Children*, 13–14.

75 Rymph, *Raising Government Children*, 14.

determinants of health and mental health."[76] It should be no surprise, then, that depression is common among impoverished mothers with young children. Eleven percent of infants living in poverty have a mother who is suffering from severe depression. This number increases to 55 percent when mild and moderate depression is included.[77] There has also been documentation that "children of parents with untreated depression have higher rates of behavior problems, difficulty coping with stress and forming healthy relationships, academic problems, and mental illness."[78]

Many researchers in this area believe the best response to this situation is to increase mental health interventions among depressed parents.[79] Although promoting access to mental health resources and mental health intervention has an important role in addressing this crisis, the primary focus should be on alleviating poverty. It is critical to focus on the underlying problem rather than wasting resources on only treating the symptoms. Furthermore, focusing solely on mental health treatment has the potentially unscrupulous effect of convincing impoverished families to accept their

76 Kevin M. Simon, Michaela Beder, and Marc W. Manseau, "Addressing Poverty and Mental Illness," *Psychiatric Times*, June 29, 2018, https://www.psychiatrictimes.com/view/addressing-poverty-and-mental-illness (accessed March 9, 2023).

77 Tracy Vericker, Jennifer Macomber, and Olivia Golden, "Infants of Depressed Mothers Living in Poverty: Opportunities to Identify and Serve," The Urban Institute, Brief 1, August 2010, 1–2, https://www.urban.org/sites/default/files/publication/29086/412199-Infants-of-Depressed-Mothers-Living-in-Poverty-Opportunities-to-Identify-and-Serve.PDF (accessed November 16, 2019).

78 Jessica Dym Bartlett, "5 Things to Know about Parental Depression," Child Trends, August 23, 2017, https://www.childtrends.org/child-trends-5/five-things-know-parental-depression (accessed November 16, 2019).

79 Bartlett, "5 Things to Know"; Vericker, Macomber, and Golden, "Infants of Depressed Mothers," 5–7.

poverty instead of streamlining efforts on addressing the economic systems that create and perpetuate poverty.

Nonetheless, terminating parental rights for reasons of poverty has been questioned by certain judges. In 1984, the Court of Appeals of Tennessee affirmed the termination of both parents' parental rights to their children on the grounds that "the conditions which led to the removal [of the children] still persist[ed]" at least one year after the removal. The parents lived in extreme poverty in a house "built from junkyard parts" with no running water. The mother suffered from cognitive delays, and the father possessed a low IQ, which limited him to unskilled work. The appeals court found that termination was in the best interests of the children. Judge Nearn dissented. He believed that although continued poor living conditions of the parents warranted continued state custody for the children, the state should not have terminated parental rights since the living situation was not willful.[80]

A few parents have succeeded in reversing TPR on appeal where poverty was the driving factor. In 2013, the Court of Appeals in Georgia reversed the TPR for a mother whose rights were terminated for failing to meet two requirements: stable housing and employment. The appeals court determined her "economic inability to provide for the children, and . . . her shortcomings in failing to comply with the two major components of her case plan stem[med] largely from her relative poverty." The court stated that "poverty alone is not a basis for termination."[81]

80 Tennessee Department of Human Services v. Riley, 689 S.W.2d 164, 165 (Tenn. Ct. App. 1984), quoted in Maren K. Dale, "Addressing the Underlying Issue of Poverty in Child-Neglect Cases," American Bar Association, April 10, 2014, https://www.americanbar.org/groups/litigation/committees/childrens-rights/articles/2014/addressing-underlying-issue-poverty-child-neglect-cases/ (accessed November 16, 2019).

81 In re C.J.V., 746 S.E.2d 783 (Ga. Ct. App. 2013), quoted in Dale, "Addressing the Underlying Issue."

In a 2008 California case where a father's parental rights were terminated because of perpetual homelessness, the appeals court reinstated his rights and noted the "absurdity" that the child welfare agency would not assist the father in obtaining housing as the state spent significant money to subsidize foster care.[82] Unfortunately, cases normally mimic the decision of the Tennessee Court of Appeals and continue to ignore the issue of systemic poverty. If parents in poverty are not lucky enough to move out of poverty, they face the risk of having their children removed and their parental rights terminated without recourse.

Studies have consistently shown the strong relationship between poverty and contact with CPS.[83] A study that took place between 1990 and 2008 discovered that each 1 percent increase in US unemployment was associated with a significant "increase in confirmed child maltreatment reports one year later."[84] In 2017, a Wisconsin study indicated that housing instability and having welfare as a sole source of income increased a family's chances of being investigated for child maltreatment among low-income families.[85]

---

82 In re G.S.R., 159 Cal. App. 4th 1202, 1205 (2008), quoted in Dale, "Addressing the Underlying Issue."

83 Margaret M. C. Thomas and Jane Waldfogel, "What Kind of 'Poverty' Predicts CPS Contact: Income, Material Hardship, and Differences among Racialized Groups," *Children and Youth Services Review* 136 (May 2022), https://www.sciencedirect.com/science/article/pii/S0190740922000366 (accessed May 27, 2022); Berrick, "Trends and Issues," 23; National Survey of Child and Adolescent Well-Being, April 2005, 6–15, http://files.eric.ed.gov/fulltext/ED501301.pdf (accessed November 14, 2017).

84 American Academy of Pediatrics, "Unemployment Linked with Child Maltreatment," *Science Daily*, October 5, 2010, https://www.sciencedaily.com/releases/2010/10/101003081452.htm (accessed November 16, 2019).

85 Kristen S. Slack et al., "Predicting Child Protective Services (CPS) Involvement among Low-Income U.S. Families with Young Children Receiving Nutritional Assistance," *International Journal of Environmental*

About half of all states have laws that specifically prohibit poverty from being the sole determination for neglect.[86] For example, the State of Wisconsin defines child neglect as follows: "Any person who is responsible for a child's welfare who, through his or her action or failure to take action, *for reasons other than poverty*, negligently fails to provide any of the following, so as to seriously endanger the physical, mental, or emotional health of the child, is guilty of neglect and may be penalized."[87] I am choosing to use Wisconsin's definition for child neglect because I am most familiar with the situation in Wisconsin. There are slight differences in definitions from state to state.[88] According to this child-neglect law, parents in Wisconsin are expected to provide necessary care, necessary food, necessary clothing, necessary medical care, necessary shelter, education, and protection from exposure to drug abuse. The law does not specify what should be done when a child is lacking a necessity because the family is in poverty.

As Roberts observes, "The definitions are vague enough to give caseworkers ample discretion to decide when living conditions amount to neglect. Very rarely do parents deliberately withhold needed resources from their children. Typically, they simply can't afford them."[89] Morales asserts, "There'll always be an excuse to remove poor kids. With almost every child they take, there is a poverty component. Once in a while, they will take a child from middle-class people. In ten years, I've come across two cases of that."[90] The situation is more alarming for impoverished Black

Research and Public Health 14, no. 10 (October 2017), https://www.ncbi.nlm.nih.gov/pmc/articles/PMC5664698/ (accessed July 20, 2019).

86 Dale, "Addressing the Underlying Issue."

87 Wisconsin Statute 948.21 (2), https://docs.legis.wisconsin.gov/statutes/statutes/948/21 (accessed July 20, 2019). Emphasis in the original.

88 Dale, "Addressing the Underlying Issue."

89 Roberts, *Torn Apart*, 67.

90 Morales, interview, March 26, 2020.

mothers with low IQs. Morales observes that "the low-IQ moms are usually quite poor. And CPS will tell the mothers that their kids will do better with parents in the suburbs than being supported by $800." Often, impoverished mothers with low IQs qualify for Social Security Disability. In the State of Wisconsin, a mother with a low IQ will receive $856 per month ($733 from the federal government and $83 from the state) as well as a $250 caretaker supplement for her first child and $150 for each additional child.[91]

President Obama's secretary of labor described the working poor in stark terms: "The typical minimum wage earner is a provider and a breadwinner—most likely a woman—responsible for paying bills, running a household and raising children."[92] Essentially, low wages seriously affect the ability of single mothers to raise their children. In addition, low wages lead to more interactions with CPS. A study that examined data from 2003 to 2013 discovered that a one-dollar increase in the federal or state minimum wage resulted in a 9.6 percent drop in neglect reports. The same study also found a significant drop in substantiated rates of neglect when the minimum wage was increased by a dollar. Studies looking at increased wages or a larger earned income tax credit for impoverished families have also illustrated a decrease in child neglect reports.[93] Money makes a difference. It aids parents in caring for their children and is also helpful in convincing potential reporters of child neglect that there is no reason to contact CPS.

Poverty is not supposed to be a reason for removing one's child in Wisconsin. Therefore, the elimination of poverty should be one of the primary paths for addressing child

91 Morales, interview, March 26, 2020.

92 Thomas Perez, quoted in Kerri M. Raissian and Lindsey Rose Bullinger, "Money Matters: Does the Minimum Wage Affect Child Maltreatment Rates?," *Children and Youth Services Review* 72 (2017): 60–70, on p. 60.

93 Raissian and Bullinger, "Money Matters," 60, 63–66.

maltreatment, but how should the CPS system respond to poverty-induced neglect when resources are not made available for families by the state or community? Some local CPS agencies have resources at their disposal to aid families suffering from poverty, but these resources are underutilized by CPS workers, who are often discouraged from providing them by agency leadership.

It is even more difficult when there are no resources to address homelessness and food security. When poverty cannot be rectified, there seem to be two options: (1) allow the children to stay with the parents or (2) permit the children to stay in foster care until the parents can obtain stable housing and food security. The CPS system seems unwilling to permit the first option. The problem with the latter option is that this opens the door for the permanent removal of the children because a judge may decide that staying with a financially stable family in the suburbs instead of their birth parents is in the best interests of the child.

The notion that a judge would decide to terminate parental rights and adopt African American children out to white families in the suburbs is not an abstract possibility. This happens all the time. In one of the case studies below, you will read about Monique, who voluntarily approached CPS in Milwaukee after becoming homeless. Instead of providing her with financial aid or a housing voucher, they removed her children and almost adopted them out. It was only the fact that she had stable housing at Casa Maria and a strong family advocate in Amada Morales that permitted her to get all of her kids back after a two-year struggle.

Financial Support for Adopters

As biological parents in poverty struggle to provide adequate resources for their children, parents who adopt the children of impoverished families will be receiving supplemental income until the child turns eighteen years old. This income, which primarily takes the form of monthly payments and medical assistance, is available to those who adopt a child with "special needs." Common sense would indicate that *special needs* refers to children with a physical or mental disability and that this would be rare among adopted children. Nonetheless, special needs in child welfare also include children meeting certain risk factors regarding disability, age, race or ethnic background, or other qualifying factors that make a child more difficult to adopt.[94]

The criteria for what determines a special-needs child vary from state to state. In Wisconsin, this designation is given to children seven years old or older, in a situation where the state is trying to place two or more siblings together, of any race except white, where there are certain genetic medical issues with the parents that could manifest in the child during childhood, to a child with inadequate prenatal care, a child who has received four or more out-of-home placements, when neglect or injury is determined during the first three years of life that could manifest in other problems later on in childhood, and on and on.[95] Based on these factors, adoptive parents may qualify for monthly payments up to two thousand dollars per month.[96]

Before seeing the list of qualifications, one might have assumed the adoption of children with special needs was more the exception than the norm, but the broad net that is cast to qualify children as special needs is obviously large. In 2016, of the 57,166 adoptions performed in the United States, 92.4 percent qualified for an adoption subsidy. In

94 Jennifer L. Lile, "Adopting a Child with Special Needs," *Special Needs Alliance*, n.d., https://www.specialneedsalliance.org/blog/adopting-a-child-with-special-needs/ (accessed March 15, 2020).

95 Wis. Administrative Code, DCF § 50.09.

96 Wisconsin Department of Children and Family, *Adoption Assistance: Information for Families*, Brochure DCF-P-PFS0105 (R. 08/2019), https://dcf.wisconsin.gov/files/publications/pdf/0105.pdf (accessed March 15, 2020).

Wisconsin, 99.7 percent of adoptions qualified for a subsidy.[97] To illustrate the growth of special-needs adoptions, 26.5 percent of adoptions in the United States were labeled special needs in 1986; this percentage grew to 42.4 percent of adoptions in 2007, and by 2014, special-needs adoptions had grown to 88.5 percent of adoptions.[98]

Perhaps the most shocking qualification listed above is that Black children—because they are not white—are considered special needs. It is very common for states to have one of their special-needs qualifications based on race. For example, in Arkansas, a white child who is at least nine years old is special needs, and so is a Black child who is at least two years old.[99] Therefore, any white person who adopts an African American child will normally receive a monthly stipend until the child turns eighteen, despite the fact that a struggling Black parent might lose their child for neglect based on poverty. The reasoning stated for counting Black children as special needs is that many Black children would not be adopted without a financial incentive.

There are two flaws with this argument. If a white couple will only adopt a Black child if there is a financial incentive, this should be a red flag that they have no business caring for an African American child. Second, this practice actually

97 US Department of Health and Human Services, "Of Those Children/Youth Adopted during Each of the FYs 2012 through 2016—Distribution of Those Receiving an Adoption Subsidy," April 30, 2018, https://www.acf.hhs.gov/sites/default/files/documents/cb/adoption_subsidy2012_2016.pdf (accessed March 9, 2023).

98 Jo Jones and Paul Placek, "Adoption: By the Numbers," *National Council for Adoption*, February 15, 2017, https://www.adoptioncouncil.org/publications/2017/02/adoption-by-the-numbers (accessed March 25, 2020).

99 Alex Ammann, "What Does 'Special Needs' Mean in Adoption?," *National Council for Adoption*, July 26, 2017, https://www.adoptioncouncil.org/blog/2017/07/what-does-special-needs-mean-in-adoption (accessed March 25, 2020).

creates a demand for adoptable Black children. One factor in a court deciding if a child should be returned home or placed for adoption is the adoptability of the child. For situations in which the court is considering the return of Black children to their parents, this practice makes it more likely that the judge will rule in favor of terminating the biological parents' rights.

The roadblocks to prevent children's reunification with their families are numerous. For example, once a child is placed in foster care, the parents lose their food stamps and the Special Supplemental Nutrition Program for Women, Infants, and Children (WIC). WIC provides "supplemental foods, health care referrals, and nutrition education for low-income pregnant, breastfeeding, and non-breastfeeding postpartum women, and to infants and children up to age five who are found to be at nutritional risk."[100] The foster parents are "automatically eligible" for WIC for any foster children they have under the age of five.[101] Depending on the state and the situation, foster parents may also qualify for food stamps.

At first glance, this seems logical. The children are living with foster parents, who should be provided help to feed them. The difficulty arises when the biological parents are granted visits with their children. At first, these visits are supervised by CPS workers, who will document the interactions for the court. If the family is living in poverty, feeding their children with a well-balanced diet is challenging because they have now lost their food stamps and WIC. Additionally, many low-income neighborhoods are food deserts without easy access to grocery stores with fresh produce.

100 US Department of Agriculture, "Women, Infants, and Children (WIC)," Food and Nutrition Service, October 17, 2018, https://www.fns.usda.gov/wic/women-infants-and-children-wic (accessed March 14, 2019).

101 "Can Foster Parents Get WIC?," Adoption.org, https://adoption.org/can-foster-parents-get-wic (accessed March 14, 2019).

If the children are infants, affording baby formula is another hurdle. The longer the children are in foster care, the more likely it is their food preferences will change, which may cause trouble feeding during the visit. Each of these factors works against a biological parent having a successful visit with their child.

Roberts believes there is a flaw in US culture that sets the groundwork for harm caused by CPS—a focus on child protection: "The child protection approach is inextricably tied to our society's refusal to see a collective responsibility for children's welfare. It is a society willing to pay billions of dollars a year on maintaining poor children outside their homes, but begrudges spending a fraction of that on supporting families."[102] David Tobis believes family preservation should be the preferred route. Nevertheless, he argues it has not had the long-term success that advocates desire because reunification programs work to "solve a family's immediate problems but . . . [do] not possess the resources to confront the larger obstacles poor families confront, such as the lack of housing or jobs."[103] He argues that CPS is able to thrive without any significant critique because "victims of poverty and racism are blamed for their condition."[104]

As Jill Duerr Berrick has stated, "US policy has long shown ambivalence toward offering substantial family support programs that might alleviate family stress and reduce the need for protective interventions. As a result, when family crises are acute, the hand of the state has always been fairly heavy and swift in its response."[105] To state it simply, US culture proposes it is in the best interests of society for

102 Roberts, *Shattered Bonds*, 89.

103 Tobis, *From Pariahs to Partners*, xxii–xxiii, 23.

104 Tobis, *From Pariahs to Partners*, xxv.

105 Berrick, "Trends and Issues," 31. See also Jill Duerr Berrick, *Take Me Home: Protecting America's Vulnerable Children and Families* (New York: Oxford University Press, 2008).

impoverished Black children to be raised outside the home rather than address racial and economic disparities.

TOLERATED PRACTICES AGAINST BLACK AND IMPOVERISHED PEOPLE

Children Removed without Proper Warrants

As previously noted, a CPS worker is supposed to obtain a warrant or a court order signed by a judge to remove a child. To protect themselves and to intimidate the parents, CPS workers in Milwaukee will normally bring a police officer with them when removing children. Many CPS workers remove children without a warrant, but the parents either do not know the CPS worker needs one or are too intimidated by the police officer to put up a fight. In Milwaukee and elsewhere, CPS workers have access to prestamped judges' orders, which they simply fill out. This is not the appropriate way to obtain a court order.

On one occasion in 2017, Amada Morales happened to be with a mother when a CPS worker arrived with police to remove her child. Morales asked to see the judges' order, but the police and the CPS worker refused to produce any documentation. At first, Amada and the mother refused to hand over the child, but they relented when the police threatened to arrest the parent. Although Morales has learned through her contacts with CPS that workers often use presigned judges' orders, it was unclear in the above situation if the worker even had that.[106] Many counties have a culture where CPS workers regularly violate protocols and laws without any consequences.

In 2019, local television and national magazine reports uncovered a similar problem in Kentucky. CPS workers

106 Morales, interview, March 26, 2020.

there had begun using presigned warrants to remove children during weekday evenings and weekends so they would not have to go through the process of meeting with a random judge who might be less familiar with the process. Even though the situation called for first getting a warrant from a judge who had reviewed the case, CPS workers kept assuming the role of the judge. In an extremely heinous instance, a judge approved the removal of one child in a family with three children, but a CPS worker used additional presigned forms to remove the other two siblings. Although defenders of the presigned warrants stated that nothing illegal was being done, the state Cabinet for Health and Family Services has now abolished the practice.[107]

Punishing Victims of Domestic Violence

For mothers facing domestic violence from a partner, the CPS system in Milwaukee adds cruelty to cruelty. When police officers are called to a domestic violence situation, they often call CPS even if children were not present at the time. This commonly results in a substantiated claim of neglect against the battered mother for the stated reason that she failed to protect her children from exposure to domestic violence. Consequently, the children are often placed in foster

107 Jason Riley, "Kentucky Workers Accused of Illegally Removing Children from Homes," *WDRB*, March 17, 2019, https://www.wdrb.com/in-depth/sunday-edition-kentucky-workers-accused-of-illegally-removing-children-from/article_5b42179c-474f-11e9-b44e-5b1688808fe4.html (accessed March 28, 2020); Breck Dumas, "Kentucky Policy Allowed Social Workers to Take Kids Using Judges' Pre-signed Signatures on Blank Documents," *Blaze*, May 8, 2019, https://www.theblaze.com/news/kentucky-policy-allowed-social-workers-to-take-kids-using-judges-pre-signed-signatures-on-blank-documents (accessed March 28, 2020); Robby Soave, "Kentucky Judges Pre-signed Blank Legal Documents So that Child Services Could Take Custody of Kids on Nights and Weekends," *Reason*, May 9, 2020, https://reason.com/2019/05/09/kentucky-cabinet-family-health-child-services-judges-pre-signed/ (accessed May 28, 2020).

care. Again, this commonly occurs even when the domestic incident occurred while the children were at school. The rationale is that the children may be harmed in the future. There are legitimate concerns that the witnessing of domestic violence can be psychologically harmful for a child, but the forced removal of a child on such grounds is unwarranted and is a situation reserved for Black and impoverished families. Removing a child from their mother only increases the child's trauma. Domestic violence calls in wealthy suburbs of Milwaukee do not result in calls to CPS.[108]

Even when the police do not call CPS, the district attorney's office may threaten to call CPS if the mother refuses to testify against the abuser. There are a variety of reasons a mother would not want to testify even if she has extracted herself from the relationship. In addition to fearing violent retaliation, she may be aware that the DA's office in Milwaukee regularly threatens the testimony of a domestic violence victim to force a plea agreement with an abuser, in which they will only receive probation. With the abuser still walking the streets, the risk created by agreeing to testify does not seem worth it. Nonetheless, it is cruel for the DA's office to call CPS when they know it could lead to child removal and TPR.[109]

If CPS is contacted, the mothers in these situations are regularly required by judges to attend a class that meets two hours every week for twenty-three weeks. You read that correctly: the victims of domestic abuse must endure a six-month class to have their children returned. The Sojourner Family Peace Center, which is contracted for these classes, states they encourage "self-sufficiency and economic empowerment for victims of domestic violence." The center was founded in 1978 as a shelter for battered women. It continues to provide needed shelter for battered women, but it also benefits financially from a CPS contract in which impoverished

108 Morales, interview, April 21, 2020.

109 Morales, interview, April 21, 2020.

mothers are required to attend their onerous twenty-three-week course or risk losing their children.[110] I wish this sort of mandated class for abuse victims was rare, but this is a common practice throughout the United States.[111]

Many mothers report their disdain for these classes. And in being forced to share their domestic violence stories before many are ready, the mothers are forced to relive traumatic events. Even hearing the abuse stories of other women can trigger a panic attack. One positive result of these forced classes is that it brings together mothers who are often isolated by the CPS apparatus. Not only do many of these mothers become support for one another regarding their CPS cases, but these classes are often also a vehicle for them to find out about people and groups willing to support them, such as Welfare Warriors and Casa Maria. In a sick twist of fate, these victims of domestic violence in Milwaukee are required to go to classes to have their children returned, while the abusers usually receive probation and are not required to attend any classes.[112]

In some cases, the children are placed in the custody of the abuser's family. In these situations, the mother has to regularly face hostility for pressing charges. Furthermore, the abuser's family has no incentive to provide a good report of interactions between the mother and her child, and in some cases, they will report an unfounded allegation of maltreatment against the mother to force her to drop the domestic abuse charges. All these factors make reunification less likely.[113]

Although no one wants children exposed to domestic violence, there needs to be a more creative solution than the

110 Morales, interview, April 21, 2020; Sojourner, "Find Safety," Family Peace Center, https://www.familypeacecenter.org/get-help (accessed March 9, 2023).

111 Roberts, *Torn Apart*, 197.

112 Morales, interview, April 21, 2020.

113 Morales, interview, April 21, 2020.

removal of the children. Furthermore, a policy that punishes the parent-victim of domestic abuse and goes so far as to remove the children discourages the reporting of the domestic abuse or the seeking of help from civil authorities or other mandatory-reporting professionals.[114] As the psychologist Lauren Shapiro and the law professor Marie-Helen Maras observe, "These practices serve to revictimize the battered parent."[115]

Charging a non-abusive parent with neglect can even affect one's livelihood. Substantiated reports of maltreatment by an adult will make that parent a "perpetrator" on the State Central Register, which is checked by employers for work involving children. As the child welfare lawyer Don Lash notes, a parent with a substantiated allegation of child maltreatment will often "be barred from whole categories of future employment, in day care schools, health care, elder care, in-home personal care, and so on."[116] This situation also happens more often to the mother-victim than a father-victim. If a father makes a domestic abuse complaint against his wife, it is more likely that only she will be charged with child maltreatment, while the father will not. There is a double standard that requires much more of mothers who are victims of domestic violence to protect their children.[117]

Court-Appointed Lawyers for CPS Cases

Unlike criminal court, lawyers are not guaranteed to parents in children's court. Whether lawyers are provided for

114 Shapiro and Maras, *Multidisciplinary Investigation*, 257. Shapiro and Maras also note, for those who point to the harm caused to children who witness domestic abuse against a parent, that studies show some children exhibit emotional, behavioral, and developmental problems, while other children do not show any negative effects.

115 Shapiro and Maras, *Multidisciplinary Investigation*, 255–60.

116 Lash, *"When the Welfare People Come,"* 3; Shapiro and Maras, *Multidisciplinary Investigation*, 258.

117 Shapiro and Maras, *Multidisciplinary Investigation*, 262.

everyone is a matter of state law and practice. In Wisconsin, lawyers are provided on request for both CHIPS and TPR cases. In Milwaukee County, county-appointed lawyers are taken from a private pool of lawyers, who had previously applied to be part of the pool. If a lawyer is part of this pool, they are typically assigned two days each month when they are supposed to show up to the courthouse to be appointed to whatever CHIPS cases begin on those days. They will then be assigned to the duration of the CHIPS hearings unless the parents ask for a new lawyer. Normally, when a parent is called into court, the lawyer will already be in the courtroom in case they are needed. If Amada Morales has had previous contact with the parents and is present that day, she will alert the parents as to which of the two available lawyers is better, and the parent can specifically request the lawyer they want. Even if they are assigned a decent lawyer who will work hard on their case, the lawyer and the parent will only be provided with the petition, or allegations against the parent, immediately before the hearing begins. This happens despite the law stating the petition must be given to each parent within forty-eight hours of removal.[118]

There is a similar private pool of lawyers for TPR cases that does not provide legal counsel for CHIPS cases. At times, public defenders may be assigned to TPR cases if they do not have any other cases at the moment. According to Morales, public defenders are usually better than the lawyers from the private pool. She has noticed that public defenders often take a "very adversarial" role against the court and seem to be more aware that allegations made against a parent cannot always be trusted.[119] This is a fundamental problem regarding the private-pool lawyers provided for both CHIPS and TPR cases. Far too many of them assume the parents have credible allegations against them and automatically

118 Morales, interview by author, May 30, 2020.

119 Morales, interview, May 30, 2020.

cooperate with the mechanisms of the CPS apparatus. In many cases, this cooperation borders on collaboration.

A parent could hire their own lawyer, but this is an unrealistic option for most since the vast majority of the parents who have their children removed are living in poverty. If someone can beg for or borrow five thousand dollars, they can find a lawyer to represent them, but for this price, they will not be a specialist in the field, and they are not necessarily more helpful than the court-appointed lawyers because of their ignorance of children's court.[120]

As previously stated, when a lawyer is appointed to a CHIPS case, the lawyer and the parent will be given the petition, or allegations against the parent, right before the arraignment hearing begins. The state and CPS caseworkers in the courtroom begin with an advantage since they already know the details of the CHIPS petition and have had time to prepare their arguments. This hearing decides if the removal of the children was appropriate. During this hearing, parents will be asked if they accept the CHIPS petition. Almost all the appointed lawyers will suggest the parent accept the petition. In doing so, the parent is agreeing to the truth and accuracy of the allegations, which often include hearsay, double hearsay, and triple hearsay. For example, an abuse allegation can come from a neighbor's cousin's friend and still be seen as credible. How any lawyer can be paid for providing such terrible and unconscionable advice is beyond understanding.

Some states, like Wisconsin, actually provide the parent with the opportunity to request a trial with a jury to dispute the allegations in the CHIPS petition, though most mothers in Milwaukee County are never alerted to this fact. Since the purpose of a trial would be to dispute the veracity of the allegations in the petition, parents are also waiving their right to a trial when they accept the CHIPS petition. The

120 Morales, interview, May 30, 2020.

acceptance of the petition will also injure their case substantially if the state later moves to terminate the rights of the parent. At that point, the opportunity to dispute the original allegations will have long since passed.[121]

Why are court-appointed lawyers so quick to have their parent-client accept the petition? The most probable reason is they do not want to create animosity in the courtroom. For many of the CHIPS lawyers, this is their only paid work. They have become well acquainted with the children's court judges and personnel. The best way to keep those relationships friendly is to go with the flow. CPS workers and judges do not want a trial about the facts of the allegations. In many cases, a trial could make CPS look bad for so easily accepting allegations, and many judges do not like the extra work. The judges are already busy with their regular caseload, and a trial is time-consuming. Additionally, a trial would require a lot more work on the part of the lawyers, most of whom seem content to be paid for doing subpar work when the allegations are weak and parents want their children back.[122]

In the State of Wisconsin, when a parent requests a trial during a CHIPS hearing to dispute the allegations in the petition, they are legally supposed to be granted a trial within thirty days. In the more than ten years that Morales has been providing court support for parents, she has never witnessed a trial happen within this timeframe. In the instances when a mother knew she could ask for a trial, she was often convinced by the judge and her lawyer that it was not in her best interest. And when she could not be persuaded, the trial would not occur for months.

If a mother can disprove all the allegations in the petition through a trial, she would have her children returned immediately, which is why the trial is supposed to happen quickly. If the trial is delayed for six months—which

121 Morales, interview, May 30, 2020.

122 Morales, interview, May 30, 2020.

is common—and the mother loses the case, then the steps necessary for her to have her child returned are delayed for six months. If a mother believes some of the allegations may be deemed credible, requesting a trial may delay the inevitable plan and requirements to be reunified with her children. Here is the catch-22: the mother may simply agree to the petition so she can begin working toward reunification, but if the court later decides to begin the TPR process, allegations from the petition—some or all of which may be false—will be used as evidence to terminate her parental rights.[123]

CASE STUDY 1: A WHITE FAMILY AS COLLATERAL DAMAGE

Although Black families are disproportionately affected by this system, white families have more children removed overall based on the greater number of white children in the United States. So even though the image of the welfare queen who cannot properly care for her children is African American, the policy decisions based on this racist projection harm many impoverished white families. In one instance, I sat with a white family in the hallway outside the courtroom for an entire day during the summer of 2019. I will call them the Robinsons.

The Robinsons consisted of a husband, wife, and teenager. They were hoping to have the two children of Mrs. Robinson's brother placed with them. The brother and his wife were both in prison for providing drugs to someone who overdosed. When the parents were initially sent to prison, CPS intervened and placed the two young children in foster care with a white couple from the suburbs. There was never any allegation of maltreatment against the parents. When the children were originally taken by CPS, the

123 Morales, interview, May 30, 2020.

social worker had called Mrs. Robinson to ask if the children could be placed with them. She told the worker she needed to consult with her husband but that she would call back shortly. When Mrs. Robinson called to state that she and her husband would gladly take the children, the social worker responded that it was too late; they had already been placed in foster care with nonrelatives.

Over the course of two years, the Robinsons had wanted their niece and nephew to be placed with them in kinship care, but the courts were slow. The Robinsons arranged visits when they could, but the foster family made visits difficult. At a review hearing held two years after the children had initially been removed from their home, the Robinsons sat in the hall outside the courtroom as the placement change contest they had filed was being heard by the judge. The judge would hear evidence and make a decision without the Robinsons in the courtroom. By then, the foster family was interested in adopting the children. The CPS social worker and the guardian ad litem advocated for the foster family. They believed the best interests of the children would be served by severing ties with the family whose relatives (the children's parents) they had labeled as criminals. Additionally, the social worker and guardian ad litem claimed the children had created a bond with the foster parents.

The Robinsons had had a child psychologist examine their visits with the children, and the psychologist testified the children still had a strong connection to the Robinsons. None of this mattered. The judge decided to keep the children in foster care, believing their adoption by the foster parents was best for them. Part of the judge's stated reasoning was that the Robinsons did not visit with the children as often as they could have. A partial explanation for this was that the Robinsons refused to visit the children at the foster parents' home with the foster parents present. Since the foster parents were hostile to the Robinsons and wanted to adopt the children, the Robinsons were rightly concerned that the foster parents would report any perceived misstep by them to the court.

The parents of the children were released from prison after two and a half years and went to court to stop the TPR, but the judge decided it was best for the kids to remain with the foster parents as they had bonded with the children, would likely adopt them, and provide them with a better life. In this example, we see a white family who lost their children without an allegation of maltreatment—in part because the assigned social worker would not wait to see if the children could be placed with relatives.

It is very common for impoverished parents to lose their children while in prison. A recent study found that 28 percent of children with open CPS cases in Wisconsin had a parent who was incarcerated. Though this is a widespread issue, we do not know the extent of the problem on a national level because this is not a statistic that is normally collected. What we do know is that mothers are more likely to have CPS involved when going to jail or prison compared to the father. And since African Americans are disproportionately arrested and sent to prison, this is an issue that imposes greater harm on the Black family. Additionally, though the criminal justice system is obligated to make inmates present for criminal court hearings, prisons are not obligated to transport parents to CPS hearings. Essentially, parents can lose the legal right to their children without having an opportunity to state their case in family court.[124]

CASE STUDY 2: RACISM AND POVERTY AS THE ONLY REASONS

An African American mother of nine turned to the Division of Milwaukee Child Protection Services (DMCPS) for help in

124 Roberts, *Torn Apart*, 208–12, 216.

October 2018. We will call the mother Monique. Monique had lost her job and became homeless. She was hoping DMCPS would provide her with a housing voucher as she searched for another job. DMCPS can provide housing vouchers when it views it as appropriate. Instead, DMCPS removed all nine children and handed the case over to Children's Hospital of Wisconsin, which then received $10,557 each month for ongoing case management. (Children's Hospital receives $1,173 per month for each child for whom they provide case management.) There was no allegation of maltreatment against Monique. She only lacked housing and asked for help.[125]

Monique's children experienced trauma from being separated from their mom, siblings, friends, cousins, aunts, uncles, and other extended family. The children were forced away from their family and community—and even each other—to be placed with multiple white foster care families in the suburbs.[126] Monique was provided the upper level of a duplex at Casa Maria so that stable housing could no longer be an impediment for reunification. Casa Maria provided housing and helped her with groceries so that she could provide meals when her children were allowed to visit. Following standard procedure, Monique lost her social service benefits, including food stamps, when her kids were placed in foster care. Even when the kids are reunified, it often takes several months before parents have their social service benefits reinstated.[127]

Monique's court conditions, activities, classes, visitations, meetings, and court hearings made it challenging for her to maintain a job, much less obtain stable housing on her own. Much of this trouble could have been avoided with little expense to the taxpayer if DMCPS had simply provided Monique with a security deposit or housing voucher from

125 Morales, interview, May 30, 2020.
126 Morales, interview, May 30, 2020.
127 Morales, interview, May 30, 2020.

their budget.[128] A year later, in October 2019, all Monique's children had finally been returned to her care, but the case would remain open for another eight months. During this time, food stamp benefits were with the foster parents, and Monique was not receiving any financial aid from Children's Hospital for any of her living expenses despite the scandalous amount of money it was "earning" from their interactions with her and her family.

During the two years that Children's Hospital worked on Monique's case, it earned $190,000 from the State of Wisconsin. If DMCPS had simply given Monique a housing voucher when she approached them and did not remove her children, the cost to the taxpayer would have amounted to less than $2,000. This money was in their budget. And though it was the unconscionable decision of DMCPS to remove the children, Children's Hospital could have advocated for immediate reunification since there was no allegation of maltreatment. To be fair, if Children's Hospital had advocated for reunification, the return of the children would not have been automatic. The decision would have been up to the judge, who would have also asked the advice of the district attorney and the guardian ad litem.[129]

The decision of the child welfare system to deny support to a struggling Black family by providing $2,000 for housing and instead to pay a "nonprofit" corporation $190,000 illustrates the total failure of this system at every level. It never occurred to the person empowered to do intake at DMCPS, or the Children's Hospital case manager, or the judge, or the guardian ad litem to advocate for keeping this Black family together at a much lower cost to the taxpayer. Furthermore, these costs do not account for the potential lifelong medical expenses that the children will face as a result of the trauma of being separated from their family.

128 Morales, interview, May 30, 2020.
129 Morales, interview, May 30, 2020.

MEDICAL INTERACTIONS LEADING TO CPS CASES

Many Black families enter the CPS pipeline after a medical visit for a child. A 2019 investigative report by NBC News and the *Houston Chronicle* documented the growth of child abuse pediatricians, "now stationed at virtually every major children's hospital in the country, [who] work closely with child welfare agencies and law enforcement, providing expert reports and court testimony in thousands of cases a year."[130] The pediatricians are presented as forensic specialists who can determine with a high degree of certainty how a child injury occurred, though being able to ascertain how by only studying the body of a child is inherently difficult. Child abuse certification for pediatricians was introduced by the American Board of Pediatricians a little over ten years ago. In 2010, there were 191 doctors certified in this new subspecialty. By 2017, this number had grown to 375.[131]

Dr. Eli Newberger, a former Harvard Medical School professor who worked in the 1970s at Boston Children's Hospital, advocates caution and humility for child abuse pediatricians. He states that "far too often," child abuse pediatricians label a situation an instance of child abuse when a more benign explanation is possible. Dr. Newberger has regularly testified on the behalf of accused parents.[132] The parents featured in the NBC News article were labeled child abusers by a child abuse pediatrician and had their infant removed. The family used their savings and borrowed from relatives to hire an expert lawyer. After spending $200,000 and proving their innocence, the case was dismissed by the judge, and CPS reversed its original findings. Because of the

130 Mike Hixenbaugh and Keri Blakinger, "Do No Harm: A Devastating Diagnosis," *NBC News*, September 19, 2019, https://www.nbcnews.com/news/us-news/devastating-diagnosis-doctors-trained-spot-child-abuse-can-save-lives-n1055746 (accessed September 22, 2019).

131 Hixenbaugh and Blakinger, "Do No Harm."

132 Dr. Eli Newberger, quote in Hixenbaugh and Blakinger, "Do No Harm."

confidentiality surrounding CPS investigations and the fact that children's court cases are closed to the public and the media, NBC News discovered "there is no way of knowing how often parents lose custody, temporarily or otherwise, based on the opinion of a child abuse doctor."[133] In this case, a white family with savings was able to get their children back. If the family had been Black and living in poverty, the outcome would probably have been different.

As reported in the far-right magazine *New American*, the African American sixteen-year-old Isaiah Rider was removed from his mother's care when she wanted to take him out of a hospital in Chicago. His mother, Michelle, had brought him to Chicago from their home in Kansas City, Missouri, to see a specialist for a painful medical condition. After an unsuccessful surgery, Michelle attempted to bring her son home, but the hospital did not want Isaiah discharged and contacted CPS. The State of Illinois soon became the legal guardian of Isaiah for the stated reason of child medical neglect. Isaiah was initially placed in foster care in Chicago but was eventually allowed to stay with relatives in Missouri. Nevertheless, the family was warned that if Michelle had unapproved contact with her son, Isaiah would be returned to Illinois. The case continued for over two years, even after Isaiah turned eighteen. He was only allowed to return to his mother's home two months shy of his nineteenth birthday.[134]

Unfortunately, the excuse of medical neglect is commonly used by medical professionals to force unnecessary treatment on children. Even if a CPS worker is sympathetic with a family's plight, it is intimidating to disagree with the professional opinion of a supposed medical expert. There are

133 Hixenbaugh and Blakinger, "Do No Harm."

134 Wolverton, "Help!," 18–19. In this internet age, Isaiah was in the unique position to plead his case to the public via videos on YouTube. His video can found by searching #SaveIsaiah.

recorded cases of school officials contacting CPS after their advice for parents to medicate their children for ADHD have been rebuffed.[135]

Below are three additional cases reporters from NBC News and the *Houston Chronicle* found to be particularly problematic:

- Three-month-old Zoey Grant's parents were concerned that a bruise on her bottom may have been caused at daycare. Since the baby could not cause the injury on her own, a child abuse pediatrician in Dallas reported the injury to CPS as an instance of child abuse by the parents. In the report, the pediatrician omitted the fact that the parents were the first to notice the injury and that they brought the child in for an evaluation. CPS workers took Zoey and her older sibling directly from their new daycare while their parents were at work. This white family with financial resources was able to hire a lawyer to have their children returned after eleven days.
- Five-month-old Mason Bright was brought to a Houston emergency room with two skull fractures and subdural bleeding. The mother stated she had accidently dropped Mason while in their driveway. A doctor in training to become a child abuse pediatrician concluded the injuries were intentional since short drops do not normally cause such harm. Later testing revealed Mason suffered from a clotting disorder, which explained the excessive bleeding. Another medical expert noted that multiple skull fractures can result from a single short fall. Nevertheless, CPS removed the boy and his older sister. This white family was not only able to get their children back but obtained a $127,000 settlement for wrongful removal.
- In another case, African American grandparents in Texas lost custody of their grandchildren and were sentenced to twenty-five years in prison. A child abuse pediatrician reported child abuse to authorities based on the pattern of burns a child

135 Wolverton, "Help!," 21–22.

received from scalding hot water in a bathtub. The Texas Court of Criminal Appeals overturned the couple's convictions in 2016, concluding the doctor "did not base his opinion on the particular facts" of the case.[136]

These wrongful child removals make parents—especially African American parents—afraid to bring their children to doctors and hospitals. The Massachusetts attorney Michael L. Rich warns, "The list of conditions that mimic abuse is lengthy" and even pediatricians can mistakenly believe a child is being abused or neglected. He recommends that attorneys in such cases "need to get every medical record of the child from birth through any pre-incident medical and hospital visits for the reported incident as well as records of medical encounters the child has had since initially interacting with CPS. The parents' medical histories are also relevant to many genetic and congenital conditions."[137]

Unfortunately, attorneys assigned to cases for impoverished families rarely take the time to conduct such a thorough investigation. When deciding whether to contact CPS, medical personnel must keep in mind that impoverished families will often be assigned poor representation. Medical personnel—and any other mandatory reporters—should not assume if they suspect child maltreatment that contacting CPS will lead to an appropriate response. Since resources are not available for most parents to clear their names, a wrongful accusation by a medical professional can easily lead to wrongful TPR. The systemic racism inherent in the US medical system has a long and well-documented history that continues today, spanning from racial bias in medical studies to unequal treatment in emergency

136 Hixenbaugh and Blakinger, "Do No Harm."

137 Michael L. Rich, quoted in Daniel Pollack, "Attorney Perspectives of Child Protective Services 'Legal Kidnapping,'" *Policy and Practice* 77 (February 2019): 24, 36.

rooms.[138] The role of racial bias inherent in the reporting of Black families to CPS also needs to be acknowledged and addressed.

Case Study in Privatization: Children's Hospital of Wisconsin

Until 1998, child welfare services in Milwaukee County were handled by the county government. In 1993, the American Civil Liberties Union (ACLU) filed a lawsuit in federal circuit court against Milwaukee County and other government officials and organizations connected to child welfare services. The suit alleged the county had failed to investigate child-maltreatment allegations, placed children in out-of-home care when other services could have preserved the family, and did not terminate parental rights when reunification was no longer an option.[139]

In response to the suit, legislation was passed on the state level in 1995 that began the process of a state takeover of child welfare services in Milwaukee County.[140] The State of Wisconsin made moves to privatize most of the child welfare system in Milwaukee County, with state workers handling the initial calls and the investigation of allegations of child maltreatment, but private contractors were utilized for any further action with the family that was deemed necessary.[141]

CPS in Milwaukee County continues to be under the oversight of the federal court system, though this may end

138 "Ending Systemic Racism in Medicine," *Nature Medicine* 26 (2020): 985.

139 Wisconsin Department of Children and Families, "Milwaukee County Child Protective Services (MCPS): Children's Rights Lawsuit," n.d., https://dcf.wisconsin.gov/mcps/childrensrights (accessed December 28, 2021).

140 Wisconsin Department of Children and Families, "Milwaukee County Child Protective Services."

141 Westat, "State Innovations in Child Welfare Financing," April 2002, 21, A–41, https://aspe.hhs.gov/system/files/pdf/72621/report.pdf (accessed May 4, 2020).

in the near future. One of the goals of this oversight was to decrease the time children spent in foster care. Children in Milwaukee County spend significantly less time in foster care now compared with the mid-1990s, but this is due in large part to increased speed in terminating parental rights and adopting out children.[142] More parental-rights terminations and quicker adoptions should not be viewed positively. When I ask people who were around before and after the privatization of child welfare services if the situation for children improved after privatization, no one has a definitive answer. One person responded, "That is the million-dollar question."

It was a rocky road for the private agencies that initially took over the primary case-management duties for Milwaukee County. In the first ten years, four different private agencies left their role as contracted case management after each one was embarrassed by a lawsuit pertaining to its mismanagement.[143] In 2004, Children's Hospital of Wisconsin acquired the Children's Service Society of Wisconsin, a nonprofit organization that had a contract for providing foster care case management and adopting out children whose parents had had their parental rights terminated.[144] Children's

142 Alison Dirr and Mary Spicuzza, "'An Important Moment': Progress in Protecting Milwaukee County's Most Vulnerable Children Means Federal Oversight Could Be Ending," *Milwaukee Journal Sentinel*, February 3, 2021, https://www.jsonline.com/story/news/local/milwaukee/2021/02/03/federal-oversight-milwaukee-county-child-welfare-could-ending/4371482001/ (accessed February 5, 2021).

143 Georgia Pabst and Crocker Stephenson, "La Causa Child Welfare Agency to Terminate Contract with State Early," *Milwaukee Journal Sentinel*, December 18, 2008, https://archive.jsonline.com/news/milwaukee/36421439.html/ (accessed March 10, 2023).

144 Julie Sneider, "Children's Hospital Acquires Child Welfare Agency," *Milwaukee Business Journal*, January 11, 2004, https://www.bizjournals.com/milwaukee/stories/2004/01/12/story2.html (accessed May 30, 2020); *Milwaukee Business Journal*, "Milwaukee County Relieved of Child Welfare Duties," *Milwaukee Business Journal*, May 30, 2001,

Hospital of Wisconsin had already had a contract to conduct medical screenings for children in the child welfare system since the mid-1990s.[145] Now, Children's Hospital is not only the largest CPS agency in Milwaukee County, with a $22 million contract and five hundred caseworkers, but it continues its role as an adoption agency. This is a conflict of interest.

If a medical opinion is needed to decide if a child is being harmed and should be separated from their parents, medical professionals from Children's Hospital of Wisconsin make that determination. When an impoverished Black child is separated from their family in Milwaukee County, the case is often handled by Children's Hospital, which receives twelve hundred dollars per child per month until the case is closed. And if the parent's rights are terminated and the child is put up for adoption, Children's Hospital will often handle the adoption and receive even more money. For Children's Hospital, there is a financial incentive to determine maltreatment, separate families, and work to terminate parental rights.[146] There is only one way for Children's Hospital to stop profiting on a case: determine that a child is safe and no longer in need of its services.

The political clout of Children's Hospital is a barrier to changes on the state level. The hospital donates to the campaigns of the top Democrat and Republican leaders in Wisconsin as well as to the campaigns of many Democrats who

---

https://www.bizjournals.com/milwaukee/stories/2001/05/28/daily12.html (accessed May 30, 2020). Currently, Children's Hospital of Wisconsin has a subsidiary that handles CPS case management, which is called Children's Family and Community Partnerships.

145 National Association of Children's Hospitals and Related Institutions, "Defining the Children's Hospital Role in Child Maltreatment," 2nd ed., 2011, 29, https://prpitx.org/wp-content/uploads/Childrens-Hospitals-role-in-child-maltreatment.pdf (accessed March 10, 2023).

146 Welfare Warriors, *Protect Children from Children's Hospital CPS Flyer* (Milwaukee, WI: Welfare Warriors, 2020).

represent Milwaukee County in the state legislature.[147] One Wisconsin legislature representative candidly told me that since their campaign receives funds from Children's Hospital, they will never publicly speak out against the hospital. If someone will not speak out against Children's Hospital, will they vote against legislation supported or authored by Children's Hospital? Will they advocate that Children's Hospital be stripped of its CPS casework and adoption contracts?

Not only has Children's Hospital of Wisconsin had its contracts regularly renewed, but it is also given free advertising money from the State of Wisconsin that is not written into any of its contracts. Each year, Wisconsin passes legislation that designates $300,000 to Children's Hospital of Wisconsin to advertise for adoptive parents at Wendy's fast-food locations in Milwaukee County. The list of sponsors for the bill in 2019 consisted of Democrats from the Milwaukee area. The bill did not pass in 2019—possibly because it was publicized by those opposing it on the Facebook pages of its Democratic sponsors.[148]

In early 2021, the bill resurfaced as part of a much larger spending bill and passed in June 2021. Casa Maria volunteers and allies worked to have this free advertising money removed from the bill, but it was more difficult to stop since it was part of a larger bill that was sponsored by a different committee.[149] Sadly, we see here another example of politicians willing to throw hundreds of thousands of dollars to help predominantly white suburban families raise impoverished Black children from the city without considering the allocation of more funds to alleviate poverty conditions.

147 Political donations to candidates in Wisconsin are tracked on this website: https://www.wisdc.org.

148 Information about this bill (AB 658–2019) can be found at https://www.billtrack50.com/BillDetail/1151569.

149 Information on this bill (SB 111–2021) can be found at https://legiscan.com/WI/bill/SB111/2021.

Children's Hospital is not the only company benefiting financially from CPS in Milwaukee County. In total, there are 169 nonprofit agencies with contracts in Milwaukee County for different aspects of the CPS process.[150] With so many contractors and subcontractors, it becomes nearly impossible to adequately assess which of these companies are doing adequate work and which are exploiting the opportunity to profit from families in desperate situations.

CPS AND AMERICANS WITH DISABILITIES ACT

Although the disproportionate presence of Black and impoverished families in the CPS system is well known, it has rarely been recognized by the courts as an unjust form of discrimination. Discrimination based on a disability is also regularly overlooked by judges in children's court. Nevertheless, the Americans with Disabilities Act provides the ability to address the unjust treatment of mothers with disabilities.

In 2015, the US Justice Department finished an investigation of the Massachusetts Department of Children and Family (DCF). The investigation revealed that DCF had "committed extensive, ongoing violations" against the Americans with Disabilities Act—specifically Title II and Section 504, which apply to government programs that receive federal assistance. Under these provisions, someone cannot be denied services because of a disability. Furthermore, government institutions cannot have policies that lead to discrimination—whether intentional or unintentional—and reasonable accommodations must be made to ensure that services are not denied to someone because of a disability.[151]

150 Pat Gowens, "Speech at International Women's Day Celebration" (speech, Milwaukee, WI, March 6, 2020).

151 Letter of Findings, Investigation of the Massachusetts Department of Children and Families by the US Departments of Justice and Health and

The Massachusetts investigation documented the case of a young woman with a mild developmental disability who had her newborn removed two days after giving birth. The removal was done as an "emergency removal" while the mom was still recovering in the hospital. The report gives her the pseudonym of Ms. Gordon. CPS denied Ms. Gordon access to family support services because they assumed she would not be able to learn how to adequately care for her baby. After her newborn was removed, CPS permitted Ms. Gordon to visit her child only one hour per week. They prohibited Ms. Gordon's mother from being present at the visits, even though the plan was always for Ms. Gordon's parents to help her with raising the child.

Based on her disability, CPS quickly decided its goal was to terminate the mother's parental rights and have her child adopted. At this point, CPS further limited Ms. Gordon to one-hour visits every two weeks. Prior to its decision to put the child up for adoption, CPS had stated reunification might be an option if Ms. Gordon worked with a parent aide during her visits to acquire better parenting skills. Ms. Gordon agreed, but CPS delayed in providing a parent aide until after it changed the goal of the case to adoption.[152]

The report chronicles several examples in which CPS failed to facilitate reunification for Ms. Gordon. In one instance, Ms. Gordon's child was crying, and she was not able to console her. CPS staff told Ms. Gordon that if she could not stop her child's crying, the visit would end, and they would take the child away. On several visits, CPS followed through with the threat by ending the visit early and removing her

---

Human Services Pursuant to the Americans with Disabilities Act and the Rehabilitation Act (DJ No. 204-36-216 and HHS No. 14-182176), 1, https://www.hhs.gov/sites/default/files/mass_lof.pdf (accessed March 10, 2023). Hereafter, this document will be referred to as "Investigation of Massachusetts."

152 Investigation of Massachusetts, 2–3, 5–6.

child. As the Justice Department report observes, the CPS workers never took time to teach Ms. Gordon, a young first-time mother with a developmental disability, how to properly console her daughter. The workers stated that it was in the "best interests of the child" to be removed when Ms. Gordon could not console her. As the Justice Department remarks, this would have been "an opportune teaching moment," but instead, the child was removed despite any legitimate safety concerns.[153]

In the two years between the removal of the child and the publication of the report, multiple experts had stated that the mother would be able to lovingly care for her child if the proper family services were offered to her. To provide a genuine opportunity for reunification, the Justice Department report required that family services be offered to the mother.[154] Though child safety is a legitimate concern, decisions about child safety must be based on "actual risks, not on mere speculation, stereotypes, or generalizations about individuals with disabilities."[155] The report continues, "Reliance on unwarranted assumptions about Ms. Gordon's developmental disability is precisely the sort of an outdated approach that the ADA and Section 504 were enacted to prohibit."[156] The conclusion of the investigation was that procedures needed to be put in place to prevent such systematic discrimination and that all investigators, social workers, family resource workers, and supervisors should be properly trained on the pertinent areas of the Americans with Disabilities Act.[157]

It would be a great help to all families if the strict requirements that the Justice Department placed on CPS in Ms. Gordon's case were applied to CPS in all cases—this

153 Investigation of Massachusetts, 21.
154 Investigation of Massachusetts, 2–3.
155 Investigation of Massachusetts, 11.
156 Investigation of Massachusetts, 14.
157 Investigation of Massachusetts, 24.

requirement being that CPS should first and foremost be a resource to help families and genuinely work toward reunification before making unjustified decisions to terminate parental rights based on preconceived notions of the families they are supposed to be serving. In Ms. Gordon's case, CPS personnel were held accountable for intentional—and unintentional—discrimination based on the Americans with Disabilities Act. If CPS personnel were also held accountable for intentional and unintentional racial bias, major changes would need to be implemented to correct the current problem.

THREE

Parental Guidance Suggested: Theological Visions of the Rights of Parents

The history and racist practices of CPS toward Black parents explored in the first two chapters have a theological foundation rooted in anti-Black ideology. I am employing a thick definition of *theological foundation* to refer to a community's most deeply held beliefs and how these cultural beliefs affect how a society is organized. This chapter contrasts the destructive theology that has led to the current manifestation of CPS with a liberative one. Using tools from Catholic Social Teaching (CST), medieval theology, and contemporary moral theology, the chapter juxtaposes the Catholic concepts of social rights and communal responsibility with the individual political rights that are protected in the United States. Far from a Catholic triumphalist stance, this chapter closes with the Catholic Church's troubled history with anti-Black racism. Although the Christian tradition has spiritual, moral, and intellectual tools for liberation, they can be coopted and corrupted if the Church is not attentive to the invasive nature of anti-Black ideology.

ROOTS OF US RACIST THEOLOGY

This section will examine the roots of US racist theology, which is the theological foundation for racist institutions like

CPS. US culture and history possess a theological notion of divinity and a corresponding human response. I propose that the deity honored in US culture is wealth and that the values associated with this deity are equality, individualism, and greed. I will be drawing from the work of Thomas Hobbes (1588–1679). Although he was an English philosopher, his thought has greatly influenced US culture.

Hobbes continued the turn toward the individual that began in the philosophy of Descartes, which placed truth in the judgment of the individual with his classic formulation "I think, therefore I am." At first glance, this appears to be a positive development that removed the overemphasis on finding truth primarily in the Christian Scriptures and the Catholic Church. But as the ethicist Joel Edward Goza argues, "Since the pursuit of 'reason' was the quest of the rich white men, once reason worked as an independent muscle what looked reasonable begins looking like the man in the mirror."[1] Though Hobbes asserted the natural equality of all human beings, he did not promote equity. Equality denotes the same basic abilities of mind and body; equity asserts that everyone should be treated fairly and given equal access to goods. In Catholic thought, the notion of equity is connected to the principle of the universal destination of goods.

Hobbes's pessimistic view of humanity as greedy resulted in the constant threat of violence and war. Oddly, the equality of human beings regarding abilities increased his fear of others, resulting in his search to sanctify greed and inequity. Hobbes accomplished this by promoting contracts over virtues. When someone is no longer concerned about Catholic virtues—which include love and justice—they are no longer concerned with protecting the dignity of the most

1 Joel Edward Goza, *America's Unholy Ghosts: The Racist Roots of Our Faith and Politics* (Eugene, OR: Cascade Books, 2018), 43. The contents of this section are deeply indebted to this book.

vulnerable.[2] Although the United States may not think of itself as greedy, income inequality is largely accepted. For example, the United States uses an outsized proportion of the world's resources without any plans to correct this inequity. Even though this country represents less than 5 percent of the world's population, it uses one-third of the world's paper, a quarter of the world's oil, 23 percent of the coal, 27 percent of the aluminum, and 19 percent of the copper.[3] This has been accomplished through military might and trade agreements.

In US society, most contracts—even unjust ones—are enforced by law. A contract has to reach an unprecedented level of injustice for a court to negate its enforceability. When someone signs a contract that harms them, the typical response from the general public is that the person should have read the small print. The contractual vision of society provides the illusion of fairness and justice. Those with the resources to draw up contracts benefit more than those who sign a contract without the resources to hire a lawyer. Furthermore, people in vulnerable situations will knowingly agree to an inequitable contract because it is the only way to survive. Examples of this include receiving a payday loan, agreeing to work for less than a livable wage, and an innocent person taking a plea bargain.

To prevent the removal of one's children, a parent without financial resources is often forced to sign a "voluntary" contract with a CPS investigator, where the parent agrees to fulfill a set of conditions and be regularly observed. When children are placed in foster care, the court will lay down a set of conditions—often onerous—that must be fulfilled before it will consider reunification. When parental rights are terminated, one often hears the refrain, "Well, she didn't

2 Goza, *America's Unholy Ghosts*, 52–53.

3 Dave Tilford, *Sustainable Consumption: Why Consumption Matters* (Oakland, CA: Sierra Club, 2000).

fulfill her conditions in a timely manner." This is meant to place the blame on the parent, as if the contract were fair and voluntary.

Perhaps the most famous example of a contract agreed to under duress is from the Old Testament. Esau gave his inheritance to his younger brother Jacob for a bowl of soup. A starving Esau arrived at home to find Jacob making lentil soup for his father. Esau begged this brother for some of his soup, but Jacob would not provide Esau with sustenance unless he renounced his inheritance. Realizing that an inheritance is useless if one is dead, Esau relented in order to survive. Jacob recognized his favorable position and took advantage of his brother.[4]

To further negate the need for equity, Hobbes promoted the idea that wealth is honorable and a sign of God's favor, while poverty is dishonorable.[5] John Locke would continue Hobbes's thought and introduce the notion of moral poverty. According to this view, poverty is not due to any societal injustice but rather the moral failings of those living in poverty. When this viewpoint is adopted, those with wealth need not feel any compunction for forcing impoverished people into exploitive contracts. It also led to Locke's justification of indentured servitude. Parents and children alike were to be sent to workhouses to "learn" the importance of work. Using a similar train of thought, Locke would justify African slavery.[6]

How does racism fit into values of equality, individualism, and greed? Since these values promote maintaining—or increasing—the wealth of rich white men, they offer no protection to impoverished people or people of color. In fact, they set the stage for exploiting those of African descent and then blaming them for it. The fear instilled by the equal ability of

4 Genesis 25:29–34.

5 Goza, *America's Unholy Ghosts*, 55.

6 Goza, *America's Unholy Ghosts*, 106–8.

"othered" individuals justifies horrific practices by those with wealth in their pursuit of maintaining power and increasing that wealth. These views were adopted by the Founding Fathers of the United States. Furthermore, the concern that England would soon abolish slavery played a substantial role in the founders deciding to break from England.[7]

For Hobbes, equality, individualism, and greed led to the justification of workhouses for impoverished people, slavery for Africans and Indigenous Americans, and genocide of nonwhite populations. And not only should no guilt be incurred by these actions, but they were encouraged as an appropriate way to build civilization.[8] Once one justifies workhouses, slavery based on race, and separating families, the current CPS structure that polices Black and impoverished families appears to be a logical development. Though the overt practices of slavery and Jim Crow have become unacceptable, CPS as a form of family policing has replaced them.

The next section will begin exploring the Catholic viewpoint on parenthood and the family as they relate to child welfare. Afterward, we will compare the values the United States has received from Hobbes with the following Catholic values by juxtaposing the rights guaranteed by the US Constitution and the rights as articulated by St. Pope John XXIII in 1963.

HISTORICAL CATHOLIC THOUGHT ON PARENTAL RIGHTS AND RESPONSIBILITIES

The dominant line of thinking in child welfare services is that the primary client in a CPS case is the child. The premise of

7 Goza, *America's Unholy Ghosts*, 64. See also Gerald Horne, *The Counter Revolution of 1776: Slave Resistance and the Origins of the United States of America* (New York: New York University Press, 2014).

8 Goza, *America's Unholy Ghosts*, 48–52, 58–59.

this argument is that only by making the child the primary client can their safety be best protected.[9] On a practical level, this is borne out with the notion of the best interests of the child. Except in exceptional cases, the traditional Catholic point of view disagrees with this thinking and underscores the rights of the parent, which it views as best for the child. This section provides a brief account of parental rights in the Catholic tradition. We examine St. Thomas Aquinas's test case for parental rights during the Middle Ages and the view of parental rights in papal encyclicals since the late nineteenth century. Although CST found in the writings of the popes does not consist of documents focused on CPS, many CST documents contend with social injustices against the family that can be redirected to this area for great benefit.

During the Middle Ages, St. Thomas Aquinas considered the question of whether the children of unbelievers should be baptized against the will of their parents. He responded in the negative, though this may seem surprising at first glance. In a society with such a close relationship between church and state, one might think Aquinas would advocate forcing the state religion on the children of nonbelievers as a benefit to the common good. Additionally, the issue took on even greater importance than the temporal common good because of the risk to the children's eternal souls of being raised outside the Christian faith. Nevertheless, Aquinas believed that to baptize the children of Jews or other non-Christians was a sin against the order set down by natural law and natural justice,[10] the injustice in this case being the termination of parental rights regarding in which faith parents will choose to raise their children.

For Aquinas, there are never exceptions for actions that are unjust. In addition to the scandal that might have been caused if Jews baptized as children returned to the religion

9 Gelles, *Out of Harm's Way*, 75–77.

10 Thomas Aquinas, *Summa theologiae* II–II, question 10, article 12.

of their parents, Aquinas believed that young children were naturally part of their parents. First, he argued this was true in a physical sense during pregnancy. Second, he believed it was also true in a spiritual sense as children were guided and formed by parents until they reached the age of reason—around seven years of age. After the age of reason, children had autonomy over certain aspects of their lives and could choose to be baptized against their parents' wishes.[11] In essence, there is a special bond between parents and children that the state should only circumvent for the gravest reasons.

In more recent Catholic thought, parental rights became a prominent issue to combat the Communist notion that the state should play a more vital role than the parents in raising children. In his 1891 encyclical on labor, *Rerum novarum*, Pope Leo XIII stated that the family was the basic building block of society, which preceded the state. He believed parents had a prepolitical right to self-determination over themselves and their children. State intervention should be rare—intervening only when the rights of a family member were being trampled by another.[12] Parental control over one's children is not an absolute, but it should be protected unless there is solid evidence that children are being seriously harmed.

Forty years later, Pope Pius XI published *Quadragesimo anno*, which updated the Church's teaching on social justice. In the document, he developed the concept of subsidiarity, which maintains that decisions should be made by the most local group possible. Unless there is a compelling reason

11 Aquinas, *Summa theologiae* II–II, question 10, article 12; Jean Porter, *Justice as a Virtue* (Grand Rapids: Wm. B. Eerdmans Publishing, 2016), 173.

12 Pope Leo XIII, Papal Encyclical, *Rerum novarum*, 13–14, http://w2.vatican.va/content/leo-xiii/en/encyclicals/documents/hf_l-xiii_enc_15051891_rerum-novarum.html (accessed July 2, 2020).

that a decision needs be created and enforced by a body not directly involved with the matter, decisions should be made by the local persons and groups affected. An example of when it is appropriate to have a local group decide a matter includes decisions about setting hours and suitable behavior for a local park. Park rules are probably best decided by the neighbors of the park, users of the park, and the local municipality. An example of a situation in which it was appropriate for a group not directly involved to override local authorities includes the federal civil rights legislation passed in the 1960s. If those laws had not been enacted on the federal level, local governments in the South would have continued in their refusal to protect the rights of African Americans. Even though civil rights legislation circumvented local legislation, it was a response to the brave actions taken by the people most negatively affected by local Jim Crow laws—African Americans.

To take the concept of subsidiarity more seriously, US society must create policies around child welfare that are informed by the voices of African Americans and those in poverty. I would suggest that policymakers sit down with parents who have had their children either temporarily or permanently removed. These are the parents who can point out the missteps in justice and policy with regard to child welfare. Perhaps a group of these parents could play a prominent role in review boards that analyze the actions taken by state and county child welfare agencies. As it currently stands, the child welfare system has not only ignored the voices of those it most impacts but it has also created an apparatus that is greatly unbalanced from a power perspective. Impoverished families and Black families do not have the resources to ensure just and fair interactions with CPS institutions or the courts, which have been supplied with plentiful federal resources and have the ultimate authority in separating them from their children.

RECENT PAPAL TEACHING ON PARENTAL RIGHTS AND RESPONSIBILITIES

St. Pope John Paul II emphasized the unique connection and relationship between parents and children: "The right and duty of parents to give education is essential, since it is connected with the transmission of human life; it is original and primary with regard to the educational role of others, on account of the uniqueness of the loving relationship between parents and children; and it is irreplaceable and inalienable, and therefore incapable of being entirely delegated to others or usurped by others." In the transmission of life, a bond between parents and children is solidified that is irreplaceable.[13] John Paul II continued:

> The State and the Church have the obligation to give families all possible aid to enable them to perform their educational role properly. Therefore both the Church and the State must create and foster the institutions and activities that families justly demand, and the aid must be in proportion to the families' needs. However, those in society who are in charge of schools must never forget that the parents have been appointed by God Himself as the first and principal educators of their children and that their right is completely inalienable.[14]

The state and the church are obligated to support families in their educating and raising of children. John Paul II was clear in stating this support should be in proportion to each

13 St. Pope John Paul II, Apostolic Exhortation, *Familiaris consortio*, 36, http://w2.vatican.va/content/john-paul-ii/en/apost_exhortations/documents/hf_jp-ii_exh_19811122_familiaris-consortio.html (accessed September 21, 2019).

14 St. Pope John Paul II, *Familiaris consortio*, 40.

family's need. For families facing inadequate access to quality housing, healthy food, and healthcare, the response cannot be to remove children from their parents. When these problems are exacerbated by racism, church and society are called to address these wrongs to support families. John Paul II specifically noted that special assistance should be provided to families facing poverty and homelessness, as well as single-parent households, families with parents in prison, and those experiencing discrimination. He advised that the response to these situations be an "even more generous, intelligent and prudent pastoral commitment, modelled on the Good Shepherd."[15]

This basic teaching was reiterated by Pope Francis in his apostolic exhortation *Amoris laetitia* (2016). He refers to the right and duty of parents to raise and educate their children. The state and its education system also have a role, but it is complementary to the primary role of the parents.[16] Regarding education, Francis explains, "The State offers educational programmes in a subsidiary way, supporting the parents in their indeclinable role."[17] Though Francis is talking specifically about education, he emphasizes that the community should offer basic support for families so that they make their own determinations. If the state has allowed systems to emerge that impoverish families to the point of children being removed, then the state has failed.

In this same document, Pope Francis draws the helpful distinction between free and voluntary acts.[18] For example, a single mother with a low-wage job may make the voluntary decision to pay the rent, even though this will result in not

15 St. Pope John Paul II, *Familiaris consortio*, 77.

16 Pope Francis, Apostolic Exhortation, *Amoris Laetitia*, 84, 259–67, http://m.vatican.va/content/dam/francesco/pdf/apost_exhortations/documents/papa-francesco_esortazione-ap_20160319_amoris-laetitia_en.pdf (accessed July 2, 2020).

17 Pope Francis, *Amoris Laetitia*, 84.

18 Pope Francis, *Amoris Laetitia*, 273.

having enough money remaining to provide nutritious meals to her children. But this is not a voluntary decision made with true freedom. Ideally, the mother would like to both pay the rent and provide nutritious meals to her children. But in the face of racism, a poor educational system, and low-wage job opportunities, she is forced to make a decision that she hopes will least harm her family.

Since CST envisions the family as the basic building block of society, which is prior to the state and given priority over the state, the state should be at the service of the family. The Vatican II document *Gaudium et spes* (1965), taking seriously the many financial concerns facing the family, states, "Serious disturbances are caused in families by modern economic conditions, by influences at once social and psychological, and by the demands of civil society."[19] Every society needs to take care to remove as many obstacles as possible that would hinder and strain the family and should install mechanisms to strengthen families so that each may have what is necessary to sustain its material and spiritual needs.

What is not often acknowledged in CST, however, is that the institution of the family is not a static reality. As with marriage and gender roles, how family is understood and defined has changed and developed. When *Rerum novarum* was published in 1891, Pope Leo XIII believed the best objective that society could provide for a family was enough land to be able to support and feed its members.[20] Such a solution seemed plausible during the 1800s because that society was more agrarian, and most people had some knowledge of farming. Nevertheless, such a solution would

19 Second Vatican Council, Dogmatic Constitution on the Church in the Modern World, *Gaudium et spes*, 47, http://www.vatican.va/archive/hist_councils/ii_vatican_council/documents/vat-ii_const_19651207_gaudium-et-spes_en.html (accessed October 14, 2020).

20 Pope Leo XIII, Papal Encyclical, *Rerum novarum*, 5–10, 47.

not address the immediate injustices confronting African American and impoverished families at this moment.

Though a guaranteed plot of land or a home to call one's own could only help in the face of homelessness and low-wage jobs, the complexities of US society require more support than a sizeable piece of land for families to flourish. In order to flourish, the average family in the United States needs a living wage, adequate healthcare, healthy food, good housing and education, transportation, internet access, and the like. Except for internet access, these needs were promoted by pontiffs during the second half of the twentieth century.[21] During the twentieth and twenty-first centuries, US society has attempted to address the growing needs of the US family with various public programs that have had varied success and unstable funding.

In two public addresses that Pope Francis gave in 2020, he proposed "basic income" as a way to combat growing poverty.[22] Also known as *universal basic income*, such a proposal would guarantee a certain monetary payment to every adult, though it may phase out if someone's income is already above a certain threshold. The attractiveness of such an idea is that it is not paternalistic because it empowers people to spend the funds on what they believe they actually need. It would also permit the elimination of other antipoverty programs, such as food stamps, welfare, housing programs, and so on. Although many of these antipoverty programs do good work, they are more often job creators for white middle-class Americans and result in impoverished people

21 For example, see St. Pope John XXIII, Papal Encyclical, *Pacem en terries*, 11–13; Pope Paul VI, Papal Encyclical, *Populorum progressio*, 6, 25, 59; St. Pope John Paul II, Apostolic Exhortation, *Familiaris consortio*, 81.

22 Nathan Schneider, "The Pope Just Proposed a 'Universal Basic Wage.' What Does This Mean for the United States," *America Magazine*, April 12, 2020, https://www.americamagazine.org/politics-society/2020/04/12/pope-just-proposed-universal-basic-wage-what-does-mean-united-states (accessed July 2, 2020).

spending countless hours of their lives waiting in line in the hopes that they may qualify.

The Catholic ethicist Thomas Massaro discerns nine key themes in CST: (1) human dignity, (2) solidarity and the common good, (3) family life, (4) subsidiarity, (5) property rights and responsibilities, (6) the dignity of work and workers' rights, (7) colonialism and economic development, (8) peace, and (9) the preferential option for those living in poverty. Although these are rich themes, their abstract nature and the Catholic Church's own propensity to overemphasize sexual and individual sins have made it difficult to instill these social teachings in the Catholic faithful and the countries in which Catholic thought could influence public discourse.[23] That being said, CST has also largely ignored racism, which is not just a US phenomenon; it is a global failing present within many countries and within the foreign policies of powerful nations toward more vulnerable nations. The relatively few references to racism in Massaro's book on the topic illustrate how the Catholic Church has been much more successful in highlighting class issues as opposed to race issues.

US RIGHTS AND CATHOLIC RIGHTS

To better understand the Catholic vision of the family, it may be helpful at this point to compare rights from both the US and Catholic perspectives. US rights are grounded in the Bill of Rights, which comprises the first ten amendments to the US Constitution. These rights are largely individual and political in nature, placing clear limitations on the government's power. These amendments include protection for the free exercise of religion, freedom of speech, peaceful

23 Thomas Massaro, *Living Justice: Catholic Social Teaching in Action*, 3rd ed. (Lanham, MD: Rowan and Littlefield, 2016), 81–124, 166.

assembly, the bearing of arms, and not being compelled to testify against oneself in a criminal case.

The Catholic vision of rights is most clearly laid out in St. Pope John XXIII's 1963 encyclical, *Pacem in Terris*. The foundational rights in this document, which largely mirror the United Nations' Declaration on Human Rights (1948), are more corporate, or communal, in nature and focus on the necessities for life. The document begins with the right to life. Building on this most basic right are "the right to bodily integrity and to the means necessary for the proper development of life, particularly food, clothing, shelter, medical care, rest, and, finally, the necessary social services . . . [including] the right to be looked after in the event of ill-health [sic]; disability stemming from his work; widowhood; old age; enforced unemployment; or whenever through no fault of his own he is deprived of the means of livelihood."[24]

The document further builds on these rights in the areas of culture, worship, economics, immigration, and politics.[25] Although many of the rights can appear to be individual in nature, they are "inextricably bound up with as many duties," which place an obligation on society to ensure that everyone has their basic needs met.[26] For instance, the right to food, clothing, shelter, and medical care depends on building a society that promotes every citizens' basic well-being.

US political rights acknowledge the equality of persons before government but do nothing to promote equity. Since the basic necessities for life are not guaranteed in the US Constitution, many people will not find themselves in a position to practice their political rights. If a mother is working three jobs at minimum wage just so her family can survive,

24 St. Pope John XXIII, Papal Encyclical, *Pacem in Terris*, 11, http://w2.vatican.va/content/john-xxiii/en/encyclicals/documents/hf_j-xxiii_enc_11041963_pacem.html (accessed September 24, 2019).

25 St. Pope John XXIII, *Pacem in Terris*, 12–27.

26 St. Pope John XXIII, *Pacem in Terris*, 28.

she will have little time to practice freedom of speech in the political realm. Furthermore, it is those with wealth in the United States who are able to magnify their speech through the purchase of ads to ensure their message is heard. Inequity, individualism, and greed lead to a situation where those who are rich are able to maximize their political rights.

Communal Responsibility and the Parable of the Good Samaritan

This sense of communal responsibility for others is epitomized in Jesus's parable of the Good Samaritan (Luke 10:25–37), where a short story is used to instill a lesson. A man is robbed and badly beaten after leaving Jerusalem on the road to Jericho. A priest and a Levite, both of whom are Jewish religious figures, pass the man on the far side of the road, keeping their distance. Then a Samaritan walks by and, overcome with compassion, tends to the man's wounds. The Samaritan brings him to an inn and pays for the man's stay until he recovers.

A common explanation behind why the religious figures passed by the victim is that touching a corpse would make them ritually impure. The Old Testament book of the prophet Ezekiel states, "They [Jewish priests] shall not make themselves unclean by going near a dead body; only for their father, mother, son, daughter, brother, or unmarried sister may they make themselves unclean" (44:25).[27] The victim on the side of the road was not a family member. And though he was not dead, they may have thought he was dead or worried he might die if they tried to move him.[28]

On the other hand, the Samaritan was despised by Jews and had no ritual purity to worry about. In fact, he may have

27 Unless otherwise noted, all translations are from the New American Bible, Revised Edition.

28 Bruce J. Malina and Richard L. Rohrbaugh, *Social-Science Commentary on the Synoptic Gospels*, 2nd ed. (Minneapolis: Fortress Press, 2003), 270.

been a trader, which would explain the wine, oil, and funds that he possessed in the parable. Traders were often wealthy, and their occupation was despised. That such a person would be the hero in the story would surprise a first-century Jewish audience.[29] Nevertheless, even this antihero recognized his responsibility to make sure the basic needs of others were satisfied.

Dr. Martin Luther King Jr. offers another perspective on this parable, on which he spoke during his last public speech in Memphis on the evening before his assassination. He began by providing a personal context for the parable, stating he and his wife had traveled on that very road during a trip to the Holy Land:

> It's a winding, meandering . . . dangerous road. In the days of Jesus it came to be known as the "Bloody Pass." And you know, it's possible that the priest and the Levite looked over that man on the ground and wondered if the robbers were still around. Or it's possible that they felt that the man on the ground was merely faking. And he was acting like he had been robbed and hurt, in order to seize them over there, lure them there for quick and easy seizure. And so the first question that the priest asked—the first question that the Levite asked was, "If I stop to help this man, what will happen to me?" But then the Good Samaritan came by. And he reversed the question: "If I do not stop to help this man, what will happen to him?"[30]

29 Malina and Rohrbaugh, *Social-Science Commentary*, 270–71.

30 Martin Luther King Jr., "I've Been to the Mountaintop" (speech, Memphis, TN, April 3, 1968), American Rhetoric, https://americanrhetoric.com/speeches/mlkivebeentothemountaintop.htm (accessed September 29, 2019).

Earlier in his speech, King contrasted the Samaritan with the Jewish religious figures by referring to him as "a man of another race."[31] It would be an anachronism to equate the definition of race in the twenty-first century with its definition in the first century. In the first century, race was not based on skin color but on one's familial country of origin. Nevertheless, the Samaritan was definitely viewed as an outsider. According to certain traditions in the Old Testament, anyone who was not Jewish would not have been considered a neighbor (see Leviticus 19:18).

Regardless of what nuance one adds to this parable, the basic message is the same: we are called to make ourselves vulnerable to help one another—even those who are not our neighbor. The philosopher Judith Butler has explored the concept of vulnerability in depth. She posits several ways in which vulnerability plays a role in fomenting and acting out resistance. A common example would be protesting in the streets. Even if someone is with others, they make themselves vulnerable to arrest, violence, and possibly death at the hands of police or counter-protesters. Those oppressed in a society are vulnerable through no choice of their own. Poverty, insecurity, and racial discrimination are common in the life of those oppressed, and this vulnerability can be a critical motivating factor in deciding to resist. Through resistance, the hope is to create a society without those vulnerabilities.[32]

Vulnerability can also be a state of mind that permits us to empathize with others. It is a willingness to accept new information in the search for new insights into lives that differ from our own. A stance of vulnerability on the part of those who are privileged is indispensable in learning about the involuntary vulnerability experienced by others. And this

31 King, "I've Been to the Mountaintop."

32 Judith Butler, "Rethinking Vulnerability and Resistance," in *Vulnerability in Resistance*, ed. Judith Butler, Zeynep Gambetti, and Leticia Sabsay (Durham, NC: Duke University Press, 2016), 12–27.

realization or conversion can lead to viewing one's culture in a new light. For those from a privileged position, vulnerability can ultimately lead to acts of solidarity, or shared vulnerability.

We are especially called to be vulnerable when the person (or people) in need is not "one of us." In the United States, our emphasis on individual rights is more akin to the question that Martin Luther King Jr. placed in the mouths of the religious authorities: "If I stop to help this man, what will happen to me?" The Catholic Christian perspective urges us to be the kind of people who ask the second question: "If I do not stop to help this man, what will happen to him?" Or to emphasize one's openness to be vulnerable, it could be restated as, "If I do not stop to help this person, what will happen to me?"

Although one could make the statement that CPS represents an impulse in the United States to care for children facing maltreatment, that statement veils the many failures of US society to eliminate racism and poverty. As previously stated, the most common type of maltreatment is neglect, resulting from poverty. The current child welfare system financially benefits the white professionals who largely make up the CPS system, along with its affiliated organizations. Impoverished families—especially impoverished Black families—are left with few resources to struggle against this system in simply trying to keep their children. Dorothy Roberts contends, "The child welfare system is designed to detect and punish neglect on the part of poor parents and ignore most middle-class and wealthy parents' failings . . . [CPS] continues to concentrate on the effects of childhood poverty, but it treats the damage as a symptom of parental rather than societal deficits."[33]

An authentic Catholic perspective promotes a corporate view of society, which sees everyone as connected to the same body. In Christian theology, this is referred to as the

33 Roberts, *Shattered Bonds*, 33.

doctrine of the mystical body of Christ (1 Cor 12–26). And just as an individual will work to restore health to a part of their body that is injured, our social body should work to restore any part of the body that is suffering. The parable of the Good Samaritan is an example of this doctrine in action. Even though the injured Jewish man was the enemy of the Samaritan, the Samaritan was moved to help him. He made a decision that his enemy should be treated as if he were a friend or a neighbor—as part of his own body.

Although the epitome of an individualist vision of US society is to be left alone, a corporate vision for society looks for a way to lift each other up so that each member may have an authentic opportunity to flourish. Ironically, impoverished Black mothers face a situation in which they cannot enjoy the ideals of corporate or individualist culture. Not only are their basic necessities ignored, but they are also not left alone. The state is an ever-present reality that regulates and constricts their lives.

SINGLE-PARENT HOUSEHOLDS

An issue that has been in the background, but not explicitly discussed, is the prevalence of single-parent households. As CST has—to a large extent—idealized the two-parent nuclear family, it seems logical that the notion of single-parent households should be addressed. Since the 1960s, there has been a dramatic increase in single-parent households. The 1960 census reported that 9 percent of children lived in single-parent households in the United States. This number steadily increased to a high of 29 percent of children living in single-parent household in the late 1990s.[34] In

34 "The Rise—and Fall?—of Single-Parent Families," Population Reference Bureau, July 1, 2001, https://www.prb.org/theriseandfallofsingleparentfamilies/ (accessed July 8, 2020).

2012, 21 million children, or 28 percent of children in the United States, lived with one parent. Statistics from the same time period indicate that of the 11.6 million single parents with children, 9.9 million were single mothers, and 1.7 million were single fathers. Where the single parent is a father, 56 percent are white, and 15 percent are Black. Where the single parent is a mother, 45 percent are white, and 28 percent are Black.[35]

Out of 130 countries, the United States has the highest rate of children living in single-parent households at 28 percent. This is four times the world average of 7 percent. In the United States, roughly the same percentage of children were born to single-parent households whether the parent professed to be Christian or stated they had no religious affiliation. In Canada, the percentage of children living in single-parent households is 15 percent. Countries whose percentage is closest to the United States are the United Kingdom (21 percent), the small Central African nation of São Tomé and Príncipe (19 percent), Russia (18 percent), and Denmark (17 percent).[36]

Along with the increase of single-parent households since the 1960s, there has been a stark increase in children being raised by unmarried parents who are cohabitating. In 1968, almost all children in unmarried households were being raised by a single mother or a single father. As of 2017, cohabitating unmarried parents made up about 35 percent

35 Yuan-Chiao Lu, Regine Walker, Patrick Richard, and Mustafa Younis, "Inequalities in Poverty and Income between Single Mothers and Fathers," *International Journal of Environmental Research and Public Health* 17, no. 1 (January 2020), https://www.ncbi.nlm.nih.gov/pmc/articles/PMC6982282/ (accessed July 8, 2020).

36 Stephanie Kramer, "U.S. Has World's Highest Rate of Children Living in Single-Parent Households," *Pew Research Center*, December 12, 2019, https://www.pewresearch.org/fact-tank/2019/12/12/u-s-children-more-likely-than-children-in-other-countries-to-live-with-just-one-parent/ (accessed July 8, 2020).

of unmarried households with children.[37] Single moms are more likely to be Black, and unmarried cohabitating mothers are more likely to be white. Although cohabitating parents are usually younger and have less formal education than single parents, the latter struggle more with poverty: 27 percent of single-parent families live in poverty, 16 percent of cohabiting-parent families live in poverty, and 8 percent of married-parent families live in poverty.[38] In the experience of the volunteer family advocate Amada Morales, she most commonly sees single parents having their children taken by CPS, followed by unmarried cohabiting parents and then married parents.[39]

Studies have shown there is a financial hierarchy among married and unmarried parents. Married parents are better off financially than unmarried cohabitating parents. And unmarried cohabitating parents are better off financially than single parents. Poverty and lower wages are concrete issues facing single-parent families. The average income of a married mother is twice that of a single mother. A large part of this is probably due to single mothers shouldering the responsibility of raising the children. This issue is exacerbated in the United States because there is no guarantee of paid maternity leave, paid sick time, or paid vacation. Additionally, being a single parent often prevents the parent from holding a standard nine-to-five job so that they can be home to watch their children when needed. Statistically, nonstandard-hour jobs pay less, are less likely to offer health insurance and pension benefits, and lead to fewer

37 Gretchen Livingston, "The Changing Profile of Unmarried Parents," *Pew Research Center*, April 25, 2018, https://www.pewsocialtrends.org/2018/04/25/the-changing-profile-of-unmarried-parents/?utm_source=adaptivemailer&utm_medium=email&utm_campaign=18-4-25%20unmarried%20parents%20press%20release&org=982&lvl=100&ite=2501&lea=561541&ctr=0&par=1&trk= (accessed July 8, 2020).

38 Livingston, "The Changing Profile of Unmarried Parents."

39 Amada Morales, interview by author, Milwaukee, WI, July 9, 2020.

promotions. Child-rearing responsibilities seem to be the biggest factor in this equation. Although married mothers earn twice as much as single mothers, there is virtually no difference in the income earned between married and single women who do not have children.[40]

As the sociologist Philip Cohen states, "You could look at this as a decline of traditional marriage, but I think it's better described as an increase in family diversity."[41] The reasons for this rapid change in family structure are debated but not known with certainty. Associated trends since the 1960s include a rise in divorce rates, people waiting until later in life to get married, and more children born out of wedlock. However, the purpose of this book is not to join the debate over why the dynamic of the US family has changed and whether this represents a moral good.

I will share one story in response to the common refrain that it is better to raise children with a mother and a father. A few years ago, I was speaking to faculty members at a local Milwaukee Catholic high school about the ethics of family life. In the midst of our discussion, a woman interjected that too many single-parent households is a problem for the school. One of the other teachers responded, "I really hate hearing that kind of remark. My father died when I was three years old and my mother had to raise me and my siblings on her own. It wasn't easy for her, but I know that she raised us just fine." I would echo the second teacher's response. Being

40 Aparna Mathur, Hao Fu, and Peter Hansen, "The Mysterious and Alarming Rise of Single Parenthood in America," *Atlantic*, September 3, 2013, https://www.theatlantic.com/business/archive/2013/09/the-mysterious-and-alarming-rise-of-single-parenthood-in-america/279203/ (accessed July 8, 2020).

41 Philip Cohen, quoted in Quentin Fottrell, "Single Motherhood in America Declines as Unmarried, Cohabiting Parents Soar," *Market Watch*, April 28, 2018, https://www.marketwatch.com/story/single-motherhood-in-america-declines-as-unmarried-cohabiting-parents-soar-2018-04-26 (accessed July 8, 2020).

a single parent can be difficult, but it should not lead to ridicule or harm. And a mother's children should definitely not be removed because she is trying to raise them by herself. Regarding the ethics of child welfare, the more important issue for US society is creating a supportive environment for all families, which will consequently aid parents in creating a healthy and loving environment for their children.

CST AND THE BLACK FAMILY

Although CST provides insights into the proper relationship between the family unit and the state, Catholic theology has a troubled history with anti-Black racism. Part of this has its origin in the time leading up to the African slave trade, when Catholic theology still accepted the morality of slavery under certain circumstances (e.g., punishment for an unjust war, capital offense, or falling into debt).[42] In 1452, Pope Nicholas V issued the papal bull *Dum diversas*, which granted Spain and Portugal "with our Apostolic Authority, full and free permission to invade, search out, capture and subjugate the Saracens, and pagans and any other unbelievers and enemies of Christ, wherever they may be . . . and to reduce their person into perpetual slavery."[43] Forty-one years later, Pope Alexander VI extended the geographical area from Africa to the Americas.[44] These statements provided religious legitimation to Catholic participation in the slave trade and to Catholic slave owners.

The Catholic Church's disturbing attitude toward Black people continued even after slavery ended. The white Catholic

42 Grimes, *Fugitive Saints*, 4.

43 Pope Nicholas V, Papal Bull, *Dum diversas*, quoted in Diana L. Hayes, *Standing in the Shoes My Mother Made: A Womanist Theology* (Minneapolis: Fortress Press, 2011), 106.

44 Hayes, *Standing in the Shoes*, 106.

theologian Katie Grimes provides a clear example in explaining the canonization of the Spanish-born St. Peter Claver (d. 1654) by the Catholic Church in 1888. Typical hagiographies about Claver state that he "labored unceasingly for the salvation of the African slaves and the abolition of the Negro slave trade, and the love he lavished on them was something that transcended the natural order."[45] Regrettably, this common interpretation of Peter Claver is far from the truth. Claver made use of enslaved Blacks in his ministry to recently kidnapped Africans arriving in Colombia. He did not oppose slavery and was known for violently beating enslaved Africans for violations against the racial public order of the time.[46] As Grimes explains, this view results in a world where white Catholics perceive Black people to be "worthy of love, but only occasionally of justice."[47] It also promotes the view that "Black resistance . . . [is] unholy, unwise, and harmful to society itself."[48]

CST has other weaknesses as well. The following ones are generalizations, but they are based on overriding patterns. First, the production of social documents by popes has been reactionary and not proactive. Each papal document was written to address a certain crisis at a certain time. In that sense, it lacks the quality of a coherent whole that can be referenced for building a more just society. Second, the documents have favored a liberal democratic capitalist system, which has often blinded them from an accurate assessment of poverty and how to address it.

Third, they have ignored the magnitude of contemporary conflicts and eschewed solutions that involve conflict. There is a naïve optimism that moral reasoning will bring

45 Hugo Hoever, "St. Peter Claver," in *Lives of the Saints for Every Day of the Year* (New York: Catholic Book Publishing Co., 1993), 375.

46 Grimes, *Fugitive Saints*, 42–44.

47 Grimes, *Fugitive Saints*, 74.

48 Grimes, *Fugitive Saints*, 75.

divergent parties into agreement. Fourth, an implicit (and sometimes explicit) patriarchal standpoint has resulted in deficient proposals for the challenges facing women in the modern world. Lastly, their emphasis on principles has made CST difficult to implement. Not only can principles be applied in widely divergent manners depending on which principle is viewed as the guiding one, but their abstract nature does not invite their contemplation by the average Catholic in the pew.[49]

Ideally, the principles in CST are supposed to lead to individual practices as well as public policies meant to promote the common good. The liberation ethics that will be examined in the next chapter share that same goal. The key difference between the two is that CST does not highlight the insights of those oppressed and rarely proposes a meaningful role for those oppressed in promoting a more just society. In fact, the guidelines and solutions proposed by CST are normally directed to the political and business leadership of a society. On the other hand, the starting point for liberation ethics is the experiences of those who are poor and oppressed, and those who are oppressed have a crucial role to play in implementing the solutions to rectify societal injustices.[50] In this sense, liberation ethics possesses a profound methodological difference from CST. Therefore, the following chapter, although complementing CST, will also move beyond it.[51]

49 María Teresa Dávila, "The Political Theology of Catholic Social Teaching," in *T&T Clark Handbook of Political Theology*, ed. Rubén Rosario Rodríguez (London: T&T Clark, 2020), 317–35, on pp. 327–28.

50 Alexandre A. Martins, *The Cry of the Poor: Liberation Ethics and Justice in Health Care* (Lanham, MD: Lexington Books, 2020), 108.

51 Martins, *The Cry of the Poor*, 104.

FOUR

The Icon of the Black Holy Family

This chapter on the Black Holy Family will augment the more principle-based CST with the biblical narrative of the nativity, which evokes a more emotional component for Christians. Although Kelly Brown Douglas rightly states that "no *one* symbol or icon can capture the presence or meaning of Christ,"[1] I would like to propose the Black Holy Family as a symbol to deepen our understanding of both the attack on the Black family in US society and the story of the biblical Holy Family in the New Testament. In figuratively painting the icon of the Black Holy Family, I will compare and contrast the historical situation of the original Holy Family with the trials faced by Black families today. Since racial prejudice based on skin color did not exist in biblical times, this comparison will not be exact, but I believe it will still be fruitful. Generally speaking, the sources for this chapter draw from the unique experience and theological reflection of Black women. This chapter would not be possible without their insights. Nevertheless, I will at times use the thought of other liberation theologians and Scripture scholars to further the arguments in this chapter.

The icon of the Black Holy Family possesses distinct advantages for confronting the racial disparity found in the CPS system. First, there is an emphasis on nondivine parents discerning the best way to incarnate God's will and bring

1 Kelly Brown Douglas, *The Black Christ* (Maryknoll, NY: Orbis Books, 1993), 108. Emphasis in the original.

Christ to others. Although God leads the way, the family is endowed with agency to follow or reject the advice of angels. Second, the Christmas story is deeply entrenched in the US psyche. There are creative possibilities for utilizing "the most wonderful time of the year" to focus on the plight of the Black Holy Family.[2] Interwoven into this chapter will be an exploration of sin, salvation, and suffering in light of our contemplation on the icon of the Black Holy Family.

The Black Holy Family was perhaps most famously immortalized in the Langston Hughes play *Black Nativity*. Near the beginning of the play, the Black Holy Family is turned away from the inn. The innkeeper does not simply state it is full but also throws insults at the family. It is insinuated they were turned away because the hotel is very refined and the family very poor. The Black Holy Family's poverty is regularly repeated, with Jesus born on an "earthen floor" with a "bed of straw."[3] In addition to Hughes, W. E. B. Du Bois wrote several stories about the modern-day Black Holy Family, including "The Three Wise Men" (1913), "The Gospel of Mary Brown" (1919), "The Sermon in the Cradle" (1921), and "The Son of God" (1933).[4] Both Hughes and Du Bois saw value in conflating the scriptural narrative about

2 Also, Marian devotion is common among Catholics. This often includes a regular practice of praying the Rosary, which is a meditative prayer on the lives of Jesus and Mary. But prayer is not meant to occur in isolation from action. Catholics with a devotion to Mary may be served by allowing their prayer life to blossom into actions that protect mothers and their children, especially families of color. Hopefully, the stories of mothers and their children struggling to stay together despite a heavy-handed CPS system will enrich the prayer life for those praying the Rosary. By learning more about the struggles facing mothers and their children today, we can delve deeper into our understanding of the troubles faced by the original Holy Family.

3 Langston Hughes, *Black Nativity* (Woodstock, IL: Dramatic Publishing, 1992 [1961]), 7, 21.

4 For a good summary of these short stories, see Phillip Luke Sinitiere, "Of Faith and Fiction: Teaching W. E. B. DuBois and Religion," *History*

the birth of Jesus with the plight of the African American family.

In *The Black Christ*, Kelly Brown Douglas directly connects biblical stories about Christ and Black women in the United States when she states that "a womanist understanding of the Blackness of Christ begins with the Black woman's story of struggle."[5] The term *womanist* was first coined by Alice Walker in her 1983 work *In Search of Our Mother's Gardens: Womanist Prose*.[6] In essence, womanist thought analyzes oppression at the intersection of race, class, and gender. It is only when the compounding evils of racism, classism, and sexism are considered together that one can compose a more accurate portrayal of the problems plaguing US society.[7]

The intersections of these oppressions, which disproportionately harm impoverished Black women, are particularly relevant for our analysis of CPS in the United States. This is relevant not only for helping to name the problem but in finding the solution. The womanist theologian Eboni Marshall Turman emphasizes the critical role Black women have recently played in Black liberation. She specifically observes that Black Lives Matter, "a movement born from the spiritual imagination and social witness of Black women, unqualifiedly asserts that the liberation power of radical self-love and justice emerges, not from the greatest among us, but from the passionate ingenuity of the least of these."[8]

Teacher 45, no. 3 (May 2012): 421–36; James H. Cone, *The Cross and the Lynching Tree* (Maryknoll, NY: Orbis Books, 2011), 104–6.

5 Douglas, *Black Christ*, 97.

6 Alice Walker, *Our Mother's Gardens: Womanist Prose* (Orlando, FL: Harvest Book, 2004 [1983]).

7 Eboni Marshall Turman and Reggie Williams, "Life in the Body: African and African American Christian Ethics," *Journal of the Society of Christian Ethics* 38, no. 2 (fall/winter 2018): 21–31, on pp. 24–25.

8 Eboni Marshall Turman, "Of Men and [Mountain] Tops: Black Women, Martin Luther King Jr., and the Ethics and Aesthetics of Invisibility in the Movement for Black Lives," *Journal of the Society of Christian Ethics* 39, no. 1 (spring/summer 2019): 57–73, on p. 70.

The Brazilian liberationist Alexandre Martins promotes the view that the suffering and hope caused by oppression provide "a hermeneutical perspective," meaning those oppressed have "a unique experience of God's revelation" that can break open new insights into Christian Scripture.[9] Martins states this experience goes beyond a psychological or religious experience to generate a new level of consciousness that directly affects how one perceives, understands, judges, and acts.[10] Although exegesis, or the scholarly interpretation of the Bible, is important, "it is not enough to understand the new message of the text in and for a new reality."[11]

Following this line of thought, the womanist theologian Renita Weems states, "Womanist hermeneutics of liberation begin with African American women's will to survive and thrive as human beings. . . . The interests of real flesh-and-blood Black women are privileged over theory and over the interests of ancient texts, even 'sacred' ancient texts. . . . The Bible cannot go unchallenged in so far as the role it has played in legitimating the dehumanization of people of African ancestry in general and the sexual exploitation of women of African ancestry in particular."[12] Weems explains that when the Bible was originally introduced to enslaved Africans in the Americas, slaveholders emphasized those passages that rationalized "slavery and oppression." Those enslaved rejected this interpretation and emphasis and interacted with the Bible from the standpoint of their own experience.[13]

Christians believe there is a liberating message inherent in the Bible. Even for non-Christians reading this book,

9 Martins, *The Cry of the Poor*, xxii, xxxii.

10 Martins, *The Cry of the Poor*, xxii.

11 Martins, *The Cry of the Poor*, xxxiii.

12 Renita J. Weems, "Re-reading for Liberation: African American Women and the Bible," in *Womanist Theological Ethics: A Reader*, ed. Katie Geneva Cannon, Emilie M. Townes, and Angela D. Sims (Louisville, KY: Westminster John Knox Press, 2011), 51–63, on p. 56.

13 Weems, "Re-reading for Liberation," 56–57.

reflecting on old stories in light of contemporary events can provide fruitful insights. As Renita Weems explains, "Stories can lure readers into seeing the world in different ways, shock them to a critique of the world in which they live and help them imagine the ways things ought to be. . . . That the Bible purports to describe ancient peoples and ancient times is part of its seduction. For even if it does not in fact describe *the* beginning of human tragedy and human triumph, it does convey to the reader the possibility that *from* the beginning of time there has been human tragedy and human triumph."[14]

Womanist use of the figure of Mary, the Mother of Jesus, is rather limited. Part of this can be attributed to the passive role that is often attributed to Mary and part can be attributed to most womanist theologians being Protestant, who place less emphasis on Mary than Catholics. Additionally, Mary has often been associated with virginity, innocence, and purity—qualities that have historically been attributed to white women in the United States to reinforce white supremacy. There are also concerns as to what extent Mary freely chose to become pregnant in the Gospel narratives. Could there be any realistic expectation that she could have rejected God's offer?[15] These are legitimate concerns that should not be casually tossed aside.

14 Weems, "Re-reading for Liberation," 60–61. Emphasis in the original.

15 Delores S. Williams, *Sisters in the Wilderness: The Challenge of Womanist God-Talk* (Maryknoll, NY: Orbis Books, 1993), 179–82. It should be noted that although Delores Williams is suspicious of utilizing Mary for Black theology, she also acknowledges that the biblical figure of Hagar, whom she offers as a resource for Black theology, also possesses challenges that make her utilization difficult. The womanist theologian Keri Day notes the invocation and emulation of Mary by the Mothers of the Disappeared to protest the murder of their children by the military government during the Dirty War in Argentina (1976–1983), but otherwise, she does not promote Mary as a model. Keri Day, *Religious Resistance to Neoliberalism: Womanist and Black Feminist Perspectives* (New York: Palgrave Macmillan, 2016), 150–52.

The Catholic womanist theologian Diana L. Hayes has responded to some of these concerns. She perceives the figure of Mary as a gift that Catholic womanists can bring to Black liberation theology. Hayes rejects the passive view of Mary and raises her up as "the symbol of . . . the courageous and outrageous authority of a young unwed mother who had the faith in herself and in her God to break through the limitations her society placed upon her to say a powerful and prophetic 'yes' to empowerment, challenging the status quo by her ability to overcome those who doubted and denied her to nurture and bring forth her son as a woman of faith and conviction."[16] Hayes observes the pattern of Mary being followed today by strong African American Catholic women who have preserved their Black Catholic heritage and passed on the faith to succeeding generations. They have done this in the midst of great struggle and suffering while keeping faith in a God "who makes a way out of no way."[17]

Echoing the above statements, I will offer a deeper understanding of the Holy Family in Scripture beginning with the Black family's story of struggle. This is why this book presented the struggles faced by modern African American families in earlier chapters before delving into theology and Scripture. This deeper understanding of Scripture in light of the Black family's struggle will in turn allow engagement with the challenges, failures, and victories of Black families in light of the Gospel stories.

HISTORICITY OF THE INFANCY NARRATIVES

The biblical sources for the Holy Family are the Gospels of Matthew and Luke, which are the only Gospels containing

16 Diana L. Hayes, *And Still We Rise: An Introduction to Black Liberation Theology* (New York: Paulist Press, 1996), 173.

17 Hayes, *And Still We Rise*, 178–79.

infancy narratives—stories about the birth and early childhood of Jesus. The infancy narratives were probably later additions to the Gospels, and their primary purpose was not to record history but rather to be "vehicles of the evangelist's [or Gospel writer's] theology and christology."[18] The earliest writings of the New Testament are Paul's letters, which provide no information about the birth of Jesus. Paul was more concerned about the death and resurrection of Christ. But as Christianity grew and became more stable in the latter half of the first century, Christians wanted to know more about the one they called Messiah. The writing of the infancy narratives also provided an opportunity to respond to criticisms facing early Christians. These likely included placing Jesus's birth in Bethlehem (also the birthplace of King David) in response to Jews skeptical of a Messiah from Galilee and emphasizing Jesus's human nature against the Docetist claim that Jesus was not actually human.[19]

The historicity of the infancy narratives is doubtful, and this can be illustrated with a few examples. First, Matthew states that Herod and all Jerusalem knew about the birth of a Messiah in Bethlehem, but no one seems to remember these events during Jesus's adult ministry, and these events are not recorded outside of the Gospels. Second, both Gospels assert the occurrence of seemingly major historical events that cannot be corroborated by any other source: the massacre of all the male children in Bethlehem and a general census of the Roman Empire by Augustus. Lastly, Matthew and Luke corroborate on very few details. In Matthew, an angel appeared to Joseph; in Luke, an angel appeared to Mary. Matthew related that the Holy Family fled to Egypt because Herod was having infants murdered in Bethlehem; Luke did not

18 Raymond Brown, *The Birth of the Messiah: A Commentary on the Infancy Narratives in Matthew and Luke* (Garden City, NY: Image Books, 1977), 26, 29–30.

19 Brown, *Birth of the Messiah*, 28.

mention this event. In Matthew, magi from the East visited Jesus; in Luke, local shepherds paid homage. The list goes on and on.[20] Or, as Scripture scholar Luke Timothy Johnson explains, "Matthew and Luke share no specific stories but only some bare information (the names of Mary, Joseph and Jesus, the place-names Nazareth and Bethlehem)."[21]

If the historicity of the infancy narratives is in question, why bother examining them? Though little in the infancy narratives may be historical fact, they are rich in theology and Christian thought. In pondering this same question, the Black liberation theologian James Cone wrote, "The mythic value of these stories is important theologically."[22] And as the biblical scholar Raymond Brown commented, "One is hard pressed to find elsewhere in the Gospels theology so succinctly and imaginatively presented."[23] If the reader of this book believes the infancy narratives are historical fact, this will not affect one's reading of this chapter. My principal purpose in examining the infancy narratives is to break open the theological and ethical implications of the infancy narratives, not quibble over historical facts. Additionally, this chapter is not an exhaustive commentary on the infancy narratives. In fact, much of the material in these narratives will not be addressed. For example, discussing the virgin birth of Jesus in Luke and Matthew does not have practical implications for the matter at hand, so it will not be discussed.

20 Brown, *Birth of the Messiah*, 32–37. Luke asserts that census took place while Augustus was emperor (27 BCE–14 CE), Herod was king (died 4 BCE), and Quirinius was governor of Syria (6–7 CE), but there was no period when these three individuals were all in their respective posts at the same time. Luke Timothy Johnson, *The Gospel of Luke*, Sacra Pagina (Collegeville, MN: The Liturgical Press, 1991), 49.

21 Johnson, *Gospel of Luke*, 34.

22 James H. Cone, *A Black Theology of Liberation* (Maryknoll, NY: Orbis Books, 2010 [1970]), 120.

23 Brown, *Birth of the Messiah*, 38.

The theologian Richard Horsley confirms the deep practical implications in the infancy narratives:

> Once freed from the both domesticating cultural context of "the holidays" and from rationalist dismissal as "myth," [the infancy narratives] can be read again as stories of people's liberation from exploitation and domination. The people who may respond most immediately are probably those whose situation is similar to that portrayed in the stories. But for modern-day citizens of "Rome," uncomfortable about their intricate involvement in the web of the new forms of domination, they also offer a challenge and inspiration to regain control of their own lives in response to God's liberation initiative in the birth of Jesus.[24]

THE THEOLOGY OF THE INFANCY NARRATIVES AND THE BIBLICAL HOLY FAMILY

The Genealogy of Jesus

Matthew's Gospel begins with Jesus's genealogy (Matt 1:1–17), which sets the tone for the rest of the Gospel: "The book of the genealogy of Jesus Christ, the son of David, the son of Abraham" (Matt 1:1). The Scripture scholar Daniel Scholz observes that in this opening line, Matthew links the identity of Jesus with two towering Jewish figures and proclaims that "Jesus fulfills the covenant that God made with Abraham and with David."[25] Luke's Gospel dramatized the genealogy by sandwiching it directly after the baptism of Jesus

24 Richard A. Horsley, *The Liberation of Christmas* (New York: Continuum, 1993), 161.

25 Daniel J. Scholz, *Jesus in the Gospels and Acts* (Winona, MN: Anselm Academic, 2009), 82.

but before he is led by the Holy Spirit into the desert (Luke 3:23–38). For both Gospel writers, Jesus's family tree had a role in properly identifying him. Even though the evangelists emphasized different aspects of his lineage for theological reasons, its importance cannot be denied. As Scholz explains, "In the first-century Mediterranean world, people were identified by their 'three G's': gender, geography, and genealogy." Matthew's genealogy connected "Jesus' roots to venerated Jewish ancestors and to key moments in Israel's salvation."[26]

Matthew's genealogy also includes four women in addition to Mary, some being foreigners and one a prostitute. The biblical scholar Daniel Harrington believes this points to "the surprising instruments that God uses, [and] the peculiar assortment of people that make up the ancestors of Jesus."[27] The Latinx liberation theologian Miguel De La Torre asserts that a serious analysis of this genealogy "forces our pietistic gaze to be taken off these women and instead focus on the historical cultures' misogynist structures that forced these women and many like them, to participate in what we have defined to be 'indecent' behavior."[28] Unfortunately, as noted in chapter 2, misogynistic attitudes still permeate our culture and reverberate throughout the child welfare system.

Harrington asserts that biblical genealogies do not necessarily contain "solid historical information." It is the function of the genealogy that is most important. In this regard, Harrington asks, "What is the genealogy saying about relationships on the domestic, political-legal, or religious level?"[29] For both Gospel writers, family history and genealogy play

---

26 Scholz, *Jesus in the Gospels*, 83, 115.

27 Daniel J. Harrington, *The Gospel of Matthew*, Sacra Pagina (Collegeville, MN: The Liturgical Press, 2017), 32–33.
Brown, *Birth of the Messiah*, 38.

28 Miguel A. De La Torre, *The Politics of Jésus: A Hispanic Political Theology* (Lanham, MD: Rowman and Littlefield, 2015), 31.

29 Harrington, *Gospel of Matthew*, 31.

a role in revealing, without limiting, their understanding of Jesus. As of June 2021, nearly forty million Americans have voluntarily taken DNA tests to find out more about their family history. This is an increase from twenty-six million Americans just three years earlier.[30] There is obviously a thirst present in the US psyche to know more about one's ancestors. There is a feeling that acquiring this knowledge will help people find out more about who they are, even though this knowledge does not define them completely.

For example, the history of Black Africans being captured and brought to the Americas during the slave trade continues to affect the lives of African Americans today. The injustice endured by their ancestors has not stopped; it has only changed in form. There can be pride and deeper self-knowledge in knowing more about one's African history—a history that includes hundreds of years of resistance to slavery and systemic anti-Black racism in the form of slave rebellions and Black liberation movements. Since many children placed in foster care are old enough to know their biological parents, it should not surprise us that one-third to one-half of foster children run away from their foster family at least once, and most of them are trying to run back home.[31]

No Room at the Inn

Luke's Gospel begins with the Holy Family living in Nazareth. They were required to travel to Bethlehem for the

30 Libby Copeland, "Genetic Testing Is Changing Our Understanding of Who Fathers Are," *Washington Post*, June 18, 2021, https://www.washingtonpost.com/outlook/dna-testing-fathers/2021/06/17/7f607c54-ce20-11eb-8cd2-4e95230cfac2_story.html (accessed March 12, 2023); Jessica Bursztynsky, "More than 26 Million People Shared Their DNA with Ancestry Firms, Allowing Researchers to Trace Relationships between Virtually All Americans: MIT," *CNBC*, https://www.cnbc.com/2019/02/12/privacy-concerns-rise-as-26-million-share-dna-with-ancestry-firms.html (accessed January 16, 2021).

31 Roberts, *Torn Apart*, 262.

Roman census. According to tradition, they were too poor to stay in a decent place, so they made do with a barn or cave meant for animals—the substandard leftovers of their society. Despite not having access to adequate living quarters, shepherds came to pay their respects. In English, the text normally states that after arriving in Bethlehem, there was no room at the inn. The New Testament scholars Bruce J. Malina and Richard L. Rohrbaugh note that the Greek word used for inn, *katalumati*, is better translated as "guest room."

In the New Testament, a different word is used for inn in other instances. The only other use of *katalumati* in the New Testament refers to the upper room where Jesus held the Last Supper (Mark 14:14; Luke 22:11). Most likely, Luke wanted to convey that circumstances would normally have obligated a family in Bethlehem to make a guest room available for a relative, even if they were not immediate family. That no one had any guest rooms available for the Holy Family indicates they were already occupied or reserved for family members "who socially outranked them."[32]

De La Torre believes Luke desired to convey the poverty of the Holy Family. He states that in the Luke's Gospel, the "manger was either a wooden box or a hole on a cave wall. The manger was the place where the cattle ate. If the barn itself was not antiseptic enough, the newborn was placed in an animal trough. In a very real sense, Jesús physically entered this world homeless."[33] Nonetheless, the main point Luke is trying to make is the same whether one believes the Holy Family was financially poor or of low social rank: this family was not valued by society at large.

The shepherds, who made a meager living, could see beyond the physical poverty and low social rank to recognize that God valued this family (Luke 1:1–20). The poverty of

32 Malina and Rohrbaugh, *Social-Science Commentary*, 375–76.
33 De La Torre, *Politics of Jésus*, 27.

the biblical Holy Family was not viewed as their own fault or a sign that God did not value them. Likewise, Black families in the United States suffer from a society that limits their opportunities for decent jobs, healthcare, education, and housing. Regardless, God still values the Black family and does not want them subjugated.

A Fearful King Herod and Systemic Sin

In Matthew's Gospel, King Herod was fearful when he heard from a group of magi that one destined to threaten his power had been born in his kingdom. The magi did not cooperate with Herod in telling him Jesus's location but instead returned home by a different route. According to this tradition, an enraged and fearful Herod had every boy two years old and under who lived in the Bethlehem area killed. But Joseph was warned beforehand in a dream to flee to Egypt to save his child's life (Matt 2:1–18). This episode reveals "the mutual threat that the child and Herod pose to each other."[34]

Although the historicity of Herod murdering all of Bethlehem's small male children is in doubt, we know Herod was a brutal, repressive, and suspicious king. Suspicious of possible assassination plots, Herod even had his two sons executed near the end of his reign. Ironically, he had initially intended them to be his successors. Though there was no proof that the sons were plotting against their father, Herod's unpopular reign had resulted in several assassination plots against him.[35] The biblical story of Herod's massacre of the children revealed his anxiety about Jesus. Jesus threatened Herod's hegemony. In a similar way, the US culture of white supremacy perceives African Americans as a threat. Whether conscious or unconscious, the white fear of Black families produces a culture and systems meant to protect white power.

34 Horsley, *Liberation of Christmas*, 23.

35 Horsley, *Liberation of Christmas*, 46–49.

Sin is often regulated to the private realm. This can be clearly seen in the Catholic sacrament of reconciliation. In the most common version of this sacrament, an individual goes to a priest, presents their sins, and expresses remorse and a willingness to do better. The priest, representing the person of Christ, forgives these sins and reconciles the person to God and community. There is an understanding that through sin, individuals not only harm their relationship with God but the community. Nevertheless, lacking in this version of the sacrament is an understanding of sin as committed by the mechanisms of society.

Sin has both individual and communal qualities. Often, sin is thought of as person A treating person B badly. Not only has person A sinned, but that sin may have communal reverberations. The sin may not only adversely affect person B but also the family and friends of the sinner, and so on. Despite the communal dimensions, the previous example is primarily an example of individual sin. We know whom to blame for the problem: person A. When the term *social sin* is used, it denotes social structures that harm a group of people within a society.

Kelly Brown Douglas defines sin as "that which alienates humans from the very ways and will of God. It is that which contests the freedom of God as a loving, life-giving force. It essentially reflects a breach with God . . . both individually and systemically."[36] In the biblical account, Herod did not directly murder the children but employed contemporary social structures to cause harm to children in the Bethlehem area. Though Herod orders these atrocities, they can only be accomplished through social mechanisms. Unlike the biblical account of Herod, no single person created the CPS system. Nevertheless, both Herod's actions and the current CPS system require the employment of a larger system. No single person can be blamed for the harm caused by CPS. It

36 Douglas, *Stand Your Ground*, 194.

has been created over generations within a culture that disdains the Black family. It is the result of social sin.

Understanding sin from a social perspective can help us recognize the harms suffered by the oppressed. Miguel A. De La Torre explains, "Recognizing the social dimension of sin lends to an understanding of sin, not from the perspective of the sinner, but from the perspective of the one sinned against."[37] In other words, an examination of social sin forces one to examine the stories of those who are suffering and to hear their voices. From this perspective, individual acknowledgment of sin and repentance "may be welcomed, but [it] remains insufficient as long as structural sins remain."[38] A focus on individual sin, individual repentance, and acts of charity do not change the structural mechanisms that cause harm.[39] Social sins, with their structural aspects, can only be remedied with changes to social structures.

There is no doubt that individual racial prejudice exists and could be confessed as a private sin. But racism and poverty are widespread problems that have become larger than the sins of a few individuals. Racism and poverty are structural and communal sins. Although the actions of privileged people today may perpetuate these sinful structures, it is often done thoughtlessly since most privileged people rarely question the culture into which they were born. This is particularly true for white people when thinking—or not thinking—about racism. The prejudicial association of Blackness with poverty in the United States makes it easier for anti-Black US culture to blame those impoverished for their poverty instead of examining social mechanisms that create poverty. And it is easier to ignore a problem when someone does not believe they had any responsibility in creating it.

37 De La Torre, *Politics of Jésus*, 152–54.
38 De La Torre, *Politics of Jésus*, 154.
39 De La Torre, *Politics of Jésus*, 157.

The Flight to Egypt

The flight of the Holy Family to Egypt is probably not historical but rather meant to evoke Jewish history. According to the Old Testament book of Genesis, Israel and his children went down to escape a severe famine (Gen 41–50). As the story continues in the book of Exodus, the Hebrews had lived in Egypt for 430 years. They had greatly increased in number but had become enslaved and horribly oppressed. The remainder of Exodus follows the liberation of the Hebrews from bondage and their journey in the desert back to their homeland (Exod 1–50).

The Holy Family's descent to Egypt and eventual return to their homeland "recapitulates [God's] people's formative history of descent into Egypt, being called out of Egypt, and coming back into the people's land still occupied by hostile rulers."[40] The Exodus event was celebrated annually during the Feast of Passover and is still celebrated by Jews today. Matthew is often viewed as promoting Jesus as a new Moses. Just as Moses was appointed by God to liberate the Hebrews from bondage in Egypt, Jesus was appointed by God to liberate humanity from its bondage to sin.

The womanist Scripture scholar Shively T. J. Smith argues that Egypt as a destination for the Holy Family should not be so easily written off as a device to have Jesus's story emulate Moses's story. Egypt was a "rich, robust, and diverse region . . . [that held an] esteemed political and cultural position in the ancient world."[41] Smith believes the importance of the Holy Family's flight to Egypt, as well as

40 Horsley, *Liberation of Christmas*, 75.

41 Shively T. J. Smith, "One More Time with Assata on My Mind: A Womanist Rereading of the Escape to Egypt (Matt. 2:13–23) in Dialogue with an African American Woman Fugitive Narrative," in *Womanist Interpretations of the Bible: Expanding the Discourse*, ed. Gay L. Bryon and Vanessa Lovelace (Atlanta: SBL Press, 2016), 139–63, on pp. 143–51.

the "extreme measures for securing survival and freedom," take on new weight when read in light of Assata Shakur's flight to Cuba.[42]

Assata Shakur is an African American exile in Cuba. For a short time, she was a member of the Harlem branch of the Black Panther Party before leaving to join the Black Liberation Army in the early 1970s. In 1973, she and two friends were stopped by New Jersey State Troopers on the New Jersey Turnpike, which Shakur has noted was "a check point where Black people are stopped, searched, harassed, and assaulted."[43] In this period without police body cameras, the exact details are unknown, but one of her friends and one of the state troopers were killed in a gun fight. In 1977, Shakur was convicted of murder and given a life sentence. Two years later, she escaped from a New Jersey prison and resurfaced in Cuba in 1987.[44]

In Cuba, Shakur has had to adjust to fewer material conveniences (e.g., hot water is lacking in certain parts of Cuba), but she appreciates the compassionate community spirit that permeates Cuba. She feels safe in Cuba as opposed to feeling under constant threat in the United States. The established Jewish communities in Egypt would have lessened the culture shock experienced by the Holy Family, but their sense of safety and security would have been similar.[45] Both of these stories defy expectations. The Jewish religious tradition has largely been defined by possessing the Jewish homeland in Palestine. But in Matthew's Gospel, the Promised Land had become a hostile environment that the Holy Family fled to survive. The United States is normally viewed by white Americans as the land of opportunity and the land of the free. But for Shakur, opportunity and freedom could

42 Smith, "One More Time," 151–52.
43 Assata Shakur, quote in Smith, "One More Time," 141.
44 Smith, "One More Time," 141–43.
45 Smith, "One More Time," 154–56.

not be found there, which forced her to flee to Communist Cuba.[46]

God's intervention to save the Holy Family also calls to mind stories of African Americans who felt compelled to flee from the South during the Great Migration of the early and mid-twentieth century. (The Great Migration was the decades-long migration [1910–1970] in which millions of Black families fled oppressive conditions in the South and settled in northern or West Coast cities.) It is also eerily similar to advice that Amada Morales gives to some moms who have gotten their kids back from CPS: "When moms tell me that they want to get out of Wisconsin after being reunified with their kids, I assure them that it's probably a good idea." She has seen CPS agencies in Wisconsin return to the same families looking for reasons to remove the children once again.[47]

The Gospel of Matthew states that after the death of King Herod, an angel of the Lord came to Joseph in a dream and told him it was safe for his family to return. At this point, the text states that when Joseph "heard that Archelaus was ruling over Judea in place of his father Herod, he was afraid to go back there. And because he had been warned in a dream, he departed for the region of Galilee" (Matt 2:22). It appears that Joseph had yet another dream in which he was warned not to return to his hometown of Bethlehem, so instead, the family settled in Nazareth in the region of Galilee. (In the Gospel of Matthew, the Holy Family is originally from Bethlehem, while in the Gospel of Luke, the Holy Family is from Nazareth but goes to Bethlehem for the census.) So even when the Holy Family returns, it is not safe to go back to their previous life in Bethlehem. Many families facing the oppressive CPS system find themselves in a similar situation; there is constant anxiety that CPS will return.

46 Smith, "One More Time," 159.

47 Amada Morales, interview by author, Milwaukee, WI, Apirl 21, 2020.

Mary's Agency and the Magnificat

An attractive aspect of the infancy narratives is the agency placed on the parents. In Luke's infancy narrative, Mary is "the principal agent of deliverance."[48] She not only cooperates with God's plan but assumes an active role, and she does all this "against the context of patriarchal social systems (that are at once political, economic, and religious)."[49] In other words, she is taking an active role against structures of social sin. The primary biblical text we will analyze to explore this claim is the Magnificat. Richard Horsley states that Mary's Magnificat is less a "pious" prayer and more a "revolutionary" song.[50]

The setting for the Magnificat occurs after Mary went "in haste" to visit her sister Elizabeth (Luke 1:39). Mary had previously been visited by the angel informing her that she would conceive Jesus by the Holy Spirit. At this point, her sister Elizabeth was six months pregnant, and Mary travels to help her during the final months of her pregnancy. At face value, the text implies that Mary traveled alone to visit Elizabeth. As the Scripture scholars Bruce J. Malina and Richard L. Rohrbaugh comment, "While travel to visit family was considered legitimate, the report of Mary traveling alone into the 'hill country' is highly unusual and improper."[51] One could speculate that Mary's concern for her sister trumped her concern to follow cultural norms for women.

The Magnificat almost interrupts the story of Mary visiting her sister Elizabeth. It may have originally been a song that existed early in Christianity that was inserted into Luke's infancy narrative. The song has its closet parallels with

48 Horsley, *Liberation of Christmas*, 81.
49 Horsley, *Liberation of Christmas*, 82.
50 Horsley, *Liberation of Christmas*, 107. The prayer is called the Magnificat because this is the first word in the Latin translation.
51 Malina and Rohrbaugh, *Social-Science Commentary*, 229.

other Jewish hymns written near the time of Jesus, including hymns found in 1 Maccabees, Judith, 2 Baruch, 4 Ezra, and the Psalms of Solomon as well as Qumran's 1QHa document and the War Scroll.[52] But other than the song likely having a Palestinian Jewish origin, we know little about its origin other than Luke found it meaningful enough to include in his infancy narrative.[53]

At this point, it will be helpful to include the Magnificat in its entirety. For most portions of the infancy narratives, it is easy enough to summarize the story. However, the Magnificat (Luke 1:46–55) is difficult to summarize; it is simply easier to present:

46 And Mary said:
"My soul proclaims the greatness of the Lord;

47 my spirit rejoices in God my savior.

48 For he has looked upon his handmaid's lowliness;
behold, from now on will all ages call me blessed.

49 The Mighty One has done great things for me,
and holy is his name.

50 His mercy is from age to age
to those who fear him.

51 He has shown might with his arm,
dispersed the arrogant of mind and heart.

52 He has thrown down the rulers from their thrones
but lifted up the lowly.

52 Horsley, *Liberation of Christmas*, 107–8.
53 Horsley, *Liberation of Christmas*, 108–10.

53 The hungry he has filled with good things;
the rich he has sent away empty.

54 He has helped Israel his servant,
remembering his mercy,

55 according to his promise to our fathers,
to Abraham and to his descendants forever."

Despite an eschatological, or otherworldly, dimension often assigned to Christian salvation, salvation in the Magnificat indicates radical changes to earthly systems. In the original Greek, Luke's verbs are placed before the subject to emphasize the actions taking place.[54] The song emphasizes God's role as a warrior savior for the vulnerable people who are oppressed. The song makes plain not only that Israel has previously been saved by God when facing desperate situations but also that Mary is a representative for the lowly. Salvation in this prayer includes a role reversal. Those who have been oppressed will be raised up, while the oppressors will be brought low and scattered. Those who have hungered for life's basic necessities and justice will be "filled with good things." This vision of God's liberating intention was promised long ago, with Luke emphasizing promises made to Jesus's ancestors.[55]

The story of salvation in Christianity is one of paradox. Christ is the savior, but he did not save the world through violence and war. He did not conquer the Romans. In fact, it was the Romans who executed him as a political dissident. Though the new kingdom proclaimed by Christ was not working to violently overthrow the Roman Empire, it was working to create a new world in the shell of the old. And for this reason, the Romans crucified Christ. Christ's

54 Horsley, *Liberation of Christmas*, 110.
55 Horsley, *Liberation of Christmas*, 110–14.

love for the world was so profound that he was willing to die for it. On the face of it, this does not sound like the story of salvation but the story of failure. The work of salvation was not his death per se but rather in the love and struggle that his death exemplified. Salvation is God's expression of love and struggle for us that is working to transform the world.

Salvation in modern Christianity is usually viewed as something personal. Street evangelists will often ask passersby, "Have you accepted Jesus Christ as your personal Lord and Savior?" But salvation in the Scriptures often takes a communal form. The Hebrew people were communally saved from their enslavement to the Egyptians. In Matthew 25, Jesus discusses the judgment of the nations at the end of time. Each nation will be brought before the judgment seat and then be separated into sheep and goats. The sheep will be composed of the communities that welcomed the stranger, visited the prisoner, and provided food for those hungry, drink for those thirsty, clothing for those naked, and care for those sick. The sheep are then brought into the kingdom of God. The goats will be composed of those communities that denied these essential goods to those in need. They are condemned to eternal punishment.[56] As in the Magnificat, the powerful will be thrown down, and the lowly will be lifted up.

56 One could argue the sheep and goats represent individuals, but nothing in the Gospel itself would indicate this. The passage does not begin by stating that all the people of the world will be gathered together but rather all the nations of the world. The Gospels are not legal documents that delineate exactly how salvation works in every situation, but both the personal and communal dimensions of salvation are present in the Gospels. According to Matthew 25, it is not expected that individuals perform each of the works of mercy as if they were a checklist, but there is an expectation that Christians work toward building communities that practice the works of mercy. If salvation can come about from working communally to accomplish the works of mercy, this communal work is also an opportunity for receiving God's grace and love.

By itself, the Magnificat could give the impression that humans have no role in salvation. It might appear to be completely the action of God. But the placement of this song in Luke's infancy narrative alerts us to the fact that Mary is not only a representative for the lowly but an active agent in bringing about God's salvation. She assents to the advice and prodding of God and God's angels to accomplish her role in salvation history. Theological debates on salvation range from an apocalyptic viewpoint that ascribes saving action almost completely to God at a future time to a realized eschatology that envisions saving action in the present by human actors. The infancy narratives do not choose either option but hold them in tension.

Karen Baker-Fletcher states, "Salvation in this life is found in communities of solidarity and resistance."[57] It is in these groups working for justice and the human flourishing of all where one catches a glimpse of salvation in the earthly realm. It is always in a state of flux and action. De La Torre draws an important distinction between salvation and justice. Justice-based actions and salvation are not the same thing, but justice-based actions are the "manifestation" of salvation.[58] He elaborates by arguing that we are saved by "justice-based praxis," which is rooted in deep listening to the Christian faith tradition from the perspective of those oppressed.[59] How one comes to acknowledge and appreciate this perspective and put it into action is a matter of grace—a gift from God to see the world in a new light. It is not something we can do on our own because of the ingrained bias that prevents us from seeing the errors of our own culture.

57 Karen Baker-Fletcher, "How Women Relate to the Evils of Nature," in *Womanist Theological Ethics: A Reader*, ed. Katie Geneva Cannon, Emilie M. Townes, and Angela D. Sims (Louisville, KY: Westminster John Knox Press, 2011), 64–77, on p. 64.

58 De La Torre, *Politics of Jésus*, 155.

59 De La Torre, *Politics of Jésus*, 158.

Similarly, in the Magnificat, God's action is the saving action that provides a new perspective and corrects injustice.

Though the language in the Magnificat betrays the patriarchal context in which it was written, the womanist theologian Courtney Hall Lee states that the Magnificat "serves as an anthem for Black women, declaring personal blessedness and worth along with intimate knowledge of God's preference for the oppressed." Lee views it in a similar vein to "the spirituals sung by Harriet Tubman as she liberated the enslaved and the freedom songs of the 1960s that were the backdrop to the civil rights movement." The Magnificat is a "freedom song."[60]

The Suffering of the Black Holy Family

Luke's infancy narrative includes the story of Mary and Joseph presenting the child Jesus at the temple. On seeing them, a righteous man named Simeon blessed the family and proclaimed to Mary, "This child is destined for the falling and the rising of many in Israel, and to be a sign that will be opposed so that the inner thoughts of many will be revealed—and a sword will pierce your own soul too" (Luke 2:21–40 RSV). The treatment of Black families in the CPS system betrays the hidden fears that white America holds for Black people. US society has opposed the Black Holy Family and has created systems to subjugate and dismantle it. When the destruction of these oppressive systems finally occurs, it will result in the falling and rising of many in the United States. But during this struggle, the hearts of many Black mothers will be pierced and suffer. In the child welfare system, the suffering of Black mothers and their children has already been extreme.

The concept of suffering in Christian thought has a turbulent past. There has been a danger in Christian theology to consider suffering for its own sake a virtue. At its worst,

60 Lee, *Black Madonna*, 118.

this has been employed to tell African Americans to happily accept their lot in society. Referring to his time as a teenager teaching Sunday School to children, James Baldwin remarked, "I felt that I was committing a crime in talking about the gentle Jesus, in telling them to reconcile themselves to their misery on earth in order to gain the crown of eternal life. Were only Negroes to attain this crown? Was Heaven, then, to be merely another ghetto?"[61]

It may be helpful to examine two very different kinds of suffering. The theologian Robert M. Doran stressed the difference between the suffering caused by victimization and "the suffering of compassion and forgiveness."[62] The first type of suffering is a private one that occurs in isolation and leaves one feeling lost. This type of suffering often leads to despair and should not be idealized. The second type of suffering occurs after one has a strong sense of self. From a Christian perspective, we may say that a person enduring the second type of suffering has experienced the healing love of God and is working to mediate God's love to others. The second type of suffering comes from a wellspring of compassion and forgiveness. Its goal is to work toward healing, reconciliation, and justice.[63]

A theology of suffering must be defined and understood only in light of resistance. Without a viewpoint of resistance, suffering could lead to "caricatures of the cardinal virtues of patience, long-suffering, forbearance, love, faith and hope."[64] These virtues must be reoriented toward freedom, which

61 James Baldwin, "Down at the Cross," in *James Baldwin: Collected Essays*, ed. Toni Morrison (New York: Library of America, 1998), 309.

62 Robert M. Doran, *Theology and the Dialectics of History* (Toronto: University of Toronto Press, 2001 [1990]), 114.

63 Doran, *Theology and the Dialectics*, 114, 244–46.

64 M. Shawn Copeland, "'Wading though Many Sorrows': Toward a Theology of Suffering in Womanist Perspective," in *A Troubling in My Soul: Womanist Perspectives on Evil and Suffering*, ed. Emilie Maureen Townes (Maryknoll, NY: Orbis Books, 1993), 151.

also is a manifestation of salvation. If freedom cannot be embodied in the here and now, it will be the goal for one's children and for one's soul. Salvation and freedom should be interpreted in light of the resurrection of Jesus. Resurrection points to a new reality and should not be confused with resuscitation. In the resurrected body of Jesus, there "is a new and different reality . . . [that] signals a new and different mode of living."[65]

The civil rights leader and former US representative John Lewis also wrote of these two types of suffering in his memoir. He referred to "redemptive suffering" as a "holy and *affective* thing."[66] This type of suffering "affects not only ourselves, but it touches and changes those around us as well. It opens us and those around us to a force beyond ourselves, a force that is right and moral, the force of righteous truth that is at the basis of human consciences. It opens and touches our hearts. It makes us feel compassion where we need to and guilt if we must."[67] But not all suffering is redemptive. Without a "graceful heart . . . [that] holds no malice toward the inflictors of his or her suffering," it is "nothing more than a sad and sorry thing."[68] Redemptive suffering requires that the sufferer has internalized the tenets of nonviolence with a view to literally "love the hell" out of their opponents.[69]

One of the most gut-wrenching examples of the suffering Black Holy Family in the twentieth century is the story of Emmett Till, the fourteen-year-old boy from Chicago who was lynched in Mississippi in 1955 for allegedly whistling at a white woman store owner. In response, the boy's mother, Mamie Till-Mobley, decided to have an open casket

65 Copeland, *Knowing Christ Crucified*, 115–16.

66 John Lewis with Michael D'Orso, *Walking with the Wind: A Memoir of the Movement* (New York: Simon and Schuster, 1998), 85. Emphasis in the original.

67 Lewis, *Walking with the Wind*, 85.

68 Lewis, *Walking with the Wind*, 85.

69 Lewis, *Walking with the Wind*, 85–86.

funeral in Chicago. Over the course of four days, tens of thousands of mourners saw his mutilated body, and pictures of the open casket were printed in newspapers and magazines. Mamie had lost her son but refused to stay silent. She even risked her own life by attending the trial of her son's murderers, who were acquitted by an all-male, all-white jury.

Mamie refused to be intimidated or silenced by the lynching. The womanist theologian Karen Baker-Fletcher interprets Mamie's actions as an example of "resurrection faith," which is "the source of power and courage to say 'No' to evil and destruction." In the midst of injustice and hate, she called for justice and love.[70] Baker-Fletcher continues, "The activist Christian faith of Mamie Till-Mobley recalls the faith of Mary, Jesus' mother, the faith of the women at the cross, the faith of the women at the tomb, and the faith of Mary Magdalene to proclaim the gospel."[71] Despite feelings of despair and suicide, Mamie refused to be "overcome by the second death that tries to take the soul."[72] A resurrection faith does not try to find meaning in these deaths or tragedies—for there is no meaning or reason to be found here—but rather find a way to restore the meaning of their lives.[73] This powerful resurrection faith helped to galvanize support for the civil rights movement of the 1950s and 1960s. Like Mamie, participants in the civil rights movement refused to be intimidated or silenced, even in the face of violence and murder.

Suffering that is incorporated into the social fabric of a society has enduring and compounding effects; this social suffering deforms the social order as it creates systems of

70 Karen Baker-Fletcher, "More than Suffering: The Healing and Resurrecting Spirit of God," in *Womanist Theological Ethics: A Reader*, ed. Katie Geneva Cannon, Emilie M. Townes, and Angela D. Sims (Louisville, KY: Westminster John Knox Press, 2011), 155–79, on p. 160.

71 Baker-Fletcher, "More than Suffering," 162.

72 Baker-Fletcher, "More than Suffering," 176.

73 Douglas, *Stand Your Ground*, 192.

"exploitation, marginalization, powerlessness, cultural imperialism, and violence."[74] Social suffering is the result of social sin, which is "bred from the cumulative and massive effect of acting from bias (i.e., perverse and self-serving individual—and group—interest), of distorting and upending crucial social values, of refusing to ask further questions or pursue additional information and insights."[75] She goes on to postulate that if the greatest evil is suffering, then the greatest good is freedom. And freedom will only triumph over suffering by more suffering that is complemented with resistance, sacrifice, and endurance.[76]

For the mothers who have lost their children to CPS, their children have not died, but they have been torn from their families and placed with strangers. The pain for the mothers and the children is real and deep. Too often, this injustice is swept under the rug and hidden. One will rightly be at a loss to find meaning in the taking away of children from their parents. There is no meaning to be found here; rather, we should focus on the love that pushes parents to resist the CPS system.

CONCLUSION

A large part of this chapter has been an attempt to expand on the notion of the Black Holy Family as presented by Langston Hughes and W. E. B. DuBois. We did this by examining the biblical Holy Family in light of the oppression facing the African American family in the United States. The wisdom and reflections of Black liberation theologians expanded this examination to include a closer look at social sin, salvation, and suffering. These theological terms can sound hollow to

74 Copeland, *Knowing Christ Crucified*, 131–32.
75 Copeland, *Knowing Christ Crucified*, 131.
76 Copeland, "'Wading through Many Sorrows,'" 136.

modern ears, but they point to tragic realities that many are struggling against.

African American families are disproportionately torn apart by the CPS system. The poverty facing many Black families as a result of generational racism is a factor, but cultural attitudes toward African Americans have also played a key role in creating unacceptable levels of "substantiated" allegations of child maltreatment, out-of-home placements, permanent placements with relatives, and adoptions. Now that we have a clearer notion of the problem, the following chapter will examine possible paths forward for salvation and freedom to break through the current CPS system of oppression.

FIVE

Paths Forward

The doctrine of the best interests of the child has been utilized to cause undue interference with Black families in the United States. As this book has shown, what warrants state removal of children varies from decade to decade and state to state. No matter the state, however, the best interests of the child in US culture have resulted in twice as many Black parents being judged as abusive or neglectful, with an even greater proportion of their children being removed from their homes. These actions have systematically worked to oppress and subjugate the Black family in the United States. This chapter will suggest acts of disruption and resistance with the aim of embracing freedom and a resurrection faith. This will be a slow and difficult process that includes suffering, but hopefully the minor victories along the way will sustain this resistance until authentic freedom is achieved.

In struggling against the CPS system, we are also struggling against a culture of racism, classism, and sexism. These cultural prejudices have led to the building of a society in which we encounter the "complexities of compoundedness" in the realm of oppression.[1] As discussed earlier, these problems are intertwined in a way that is termed *intersectionality*. Racism, classism, and sexism each has its unique attributes, but they also reinforce one another and form unique oppressions. A comprehensive response to the harm caused by the

1 Crenshaw, "Demarginalizing the Intersection," 166.

CPS system needs to address all three. Although this chapter will offer proposals to confront the injustices inherent in CPS, the truth is these problems will never completely disappear until racism, classism, and sexism have been eradicated from our cultural milieu.

When there are laws in the United States that contribute to injustice, it is logical to assume that one should focus one's resources on changing these laws. Unfortunately, significant changes to the laws guiding the CPS system seem improbable at the moment. There are several reasons for this. First, many private corporations and nonprofits benefit financially from the CPS system, whether they are contracted with case management or classes for parents who have been accused of neglect. These same companies provide significant donations to the political campaigns of Democrats and Republicans. Until there is a critical mass among the US public that is interested in changes to CPS laws, the status quo will remain. Just as no politician wants to be seen as soft on crime, no politician wants to be seen as soft on child abusers.

Second, when an accusation has been made against someone, it seems to be part of human nature to believe it is probably true. When this aspect of human nature is combined with a rightful abhorrence of child abuse, building support for a group of parents who have been accused of child maltreatment is already an uphill battle. When the culture of anti-Black racism in the United States is added to the issue, it becomes easier for the public to believe these wretched accusations against the Black family.

The Christian ethicist Traci C. West highlights the importance of bureaucratic reforms in achieving advances in the ethical practices of systemic racism. Nevertheless, she also recognizes that in bureaucratic reform, "conflict is immediately absorbed and neutralized in administrative language or procedures, such as a task force on racism, the mandatory diversity workshop, or the annual women's day worship service."[2] West asserts that lasting change requires a social movement with "repeated, direct confrontations between individuals and groups from diverse sectors of our communities."[3] In a similar vein, she acknowledges the important role that nonprofits and other organizations can play in promoting liberation, but these institutions can also fall prey to promoting inequalities, internal hierarchies, and an overemphasis on self-maintenance. Social movements, while participating in and with organizations, must be careful to remain distinct so as to still represent the communities they are working to liberate.[4]

Meaningful changes to the laws guiding the CPS system, resulting in authentic freedom for the Black family, will not be initiated by government officials. Change will only come with the insistence of parents, children, and activists supporting systemic changes grounded in racial justice. Ungirding all of the possible responses below is the refusal to be silent. In 1970, James Baldwin wrote, "Since we live in an age in which silence is not only criminal but suicidal, I have been making as much noise as I can."[5]

Since radical changes to the CPS system are probably a distant dream, Tobis recommends a multipronged strategy:

> Activists can't be certain at the outset what activities will make a difference in the short-term and what will take root in the longer term. It is therefore important to work for reforms on many fronts—conducting research, improving service

2 Traci C. West, *Wounds of the Spirit: Black Women, Violence, and Resistance Ethics* (New York: NYU Press, 1999), 191.

3 West, *Wounds of the Spirit*, 191.

4 West, *Wounds of the Spirit*, 192.

5 James Baldwin, "An Open Letter to My Sister, Miss Angela Davis," November 19, 1970, in *The New York Review of Books*, January 7, 1971, 37, https://www.nybooks.com/articles/1971/01/07/an-open-letter-to-my-sister-miss-angela-davis/ (accessed September 5, 2019).

> delivery, pressing for policy reform, carrying out grass-roots organizing, demonstrating in the street, and filing law suits. These activities should be undertaken with many different partners both inside and outside of the system—activists, academics, administrators, and service providers. Since it is often unknown who will be allies and what will work, it is important to be experimental, to take risks, and to see what strategies gain traction with different parts of the community.[6]

Many of the proposals in this chapter can only be viewed as short-term and transitory. As Vincent Lloyd and Andrew Prevot assert concerning racial inequality in the United States, "Unless this disease is named and addressed, whatever remedies are offered for the specific forms of oppression faced by Black Americans today will prove to be no more than short-term solutions."[7] In cases in which authentic freedom seems possible, the response should focus on eliminating or transforming oppressive systems. As we will see below, there is a mixture of survival responses, short-term strategies, and long-term strategies. Survival responses should be promoted where short-term change is unlikely, and pushes for short-term changes should be promoted where systemic change is viewed as unlikely. Given the complexity of reality, a combination of survival, short-term, and long-term tactics will likely be applied to most situations. A detailed blueprint for long-term changes that are unlikely in the near future is unhelpful as well as a waste of limited time and resources.

Nevertheless, dreaming a new future is a Christian necessity that aids us in uncovering social evils and revealing

6 Tobis, *From Pariahs to Partners*, 80.

7 Vincent W. Lloyd and Andrew Prevot, introduction to *Anti-Blackness and Christian Ethics*, ed. Vincent W. Lloyd and Andrew Prevot (Maryknoll, NY: Orbis Books, 2017), xv–xxx, at xxi.

paths to authentic freedom. Therefore, this chapter begins by promoting a new narrative to combat the anti-Black narrative that currently dominates US culture. Next, the necessity of supporting impoverished families is examined along with a critique of the financial incentives within CPS. This will be followed by a discussion of what the abolition of CPS, or CPS abolition, would look like and entail. We will then explore the possibilities of the collaborative approach and more training for those involved in CPS. Lastly, we will survey other proposals that do not fit neatly into the above categories.

TELLING ANOTHER STORY

Don Lash notes the need for a counternarrative. The current narrative follows the thought of Hobbes and blames impoverished parents for not properly feeding, clothing, and housing their children. Even worse, it views Black parents as a danger to their children. In this narrative, parents are either personally accountable and need to correct their behavior, or they are suffering from a pathology and need to seek treatment. Neither assessment accounts for a broken society that fails to support families economically. All too often, the CPS doctrine of the best interests of the child is employed to remove children from their parents and terminate parental rights. Lash believes this narrative is reinforced through mandatory reporting laws, which ask medical professionals, schoolteachers, police officers, and others to always be on the lookout for dangerous Black parents.[8]

One purpose of this book has been to suggest as a counternarrative the icon of the Black Holy Family. The previous chapter painted the icon of the Black Holy Family, and I believe this icon can serve as a counternarrative that recognizes the US Black family is in hostile territory, facing threats

8 Lash, *"When the Welfare People Come,"* 153–56.

and punishments simply for being Black. This assault on the Black family occurs in government policy, at traffic stops, in housing and employment, at hospitals, and in classrooms and courtrooms. These assaults compound one another and form a systemic web that promotes social sin. We have focused on how the United States' anti-Black culture has disrupted the Black family. In addition to the unwarranted suffering faced by Black families in the CPS system, we have also heard many stories of resistance. Some of these actions have been successful, and others have failed, but all have been marked by great love for one's children. This parental love mirrors the love Joseph and Mary expressed for Jesus during the many trials they faced as a family.

What would it mean for the icon of the Black Holy Family to become meaningful in the US Christian psyche? How do church and society convey proper respect and reverence for a family unit whose treatment by society reveals US culture to be anti-Black? At a minimum, it requires a change in how CPS interacts with Black families. It also requires those with vision to work for this change. Any proposals to address the injustices faced by parents in the CPS system must also address racism. So-called colorblind solutions that only address classism will not eliminate racial disproportionality. Although it is possible that solutions addressing poverty may decrease the numbers of white and Black children removed from their families, we would still have a system that treats African Americans families unfairly and harms them disproportionately.

For example, parent advocates were introduced into New York City's CPS system as a measure to provide support to parents. This program was largely responsible for the number of children in foster care dropping from fifty thousand in 1992 to fourteen thousand twenty years later.[9] Nevertheless, Black children are still disproportionately placed in foster care compared with white children in New

9 Tobis, *From Pariahs to Partners*, xix.

York City.[10] The parent-advocate program focused more on addressing the class issue of fewer resources being available for parents living in poverty but never made racial disparities in foster care a key component of its program. It should not surprise anyone that racial disparities will remain if racism is not addressed when creating such a program.

A recent example of this colorblind mentality occurred in Wisconsin in 2017. In response to the opioid crisis increasing child placement in foster care, Wisconsin created a bipartisan task force to address the issue. Unfortunately, the task force did not address the issue of racism within the opioid crisis.[11] African Americans have less accessibility to healthcare compared with whites, and African Americans are less likely to receive appropriate treatment because of the racial bias of physicians who often view their Black patients as dishonest.[12] So even though this bipartisan effort to address the effect of the opioid crisis on the CPS system in Wisconsin has been highly praised, it is unlikely to produce significant results for Black parents who still struggle to receive proper treatment for their addiction.

One of the purposes of this book has been to share another viewpoint by sharing the stories of families resisting CPS. But these lesser-known stories need to be shared more broadly. In an ideal world, these mothers would contact state and federal lawmakers, tell their stories, and expect that needed changes in the law would occur during the next

10 Tobis, *From Pariahs to Partners*, 24–25, 183.

11 Natalie Goodnow and Will Flanders, "Flooding the System: A Study of Opioids and Out-of-Home Care in Wisconsin," *Wisconsin Institute of Law and Liberty*, February 2018, https://will-law.org/wp-content/uploads/2021/01/flooding-the-system_opioids-and-ohc_final-1.pdf (accessed March 13, 2023).

12 Krystina Murray, "Racial Disparities in Opioid Addiction Treatment in Black and White Populations," *Addiction Center*, October 15, 2019, https://www.addictioncenter.com/news/2019/10/racial-disparities-opioid-addiction-treatment/ (accessed July 31, 2020).

legislative session. As the womanist theologian Keri Day reminds readers, "Poor women of color around the world are often locked out of the dominant public/political sphere where institutional policymaking occurs." Even if these women are not literally locked out, other powerful forces in society drown out their voices at the policymaking level. There is need for these mothers to create their own public spaces through protest, marches, chants, prayers, and the like.[13] Public spaces created through organized resistance allow the story of the oppressed to break through the static and enter public and political consciousness.

How a group determines a method of organized resistance is based on its talents and social circumstances. What worked in one place at a certain time is no guarantee that the same method will work in another place or time. Discovering which method to employ will require prayer, discernment, and discussion as well as trial and error. The remainder of this section will explore possible goals to be achieved if one can break through the static that currently clouds US political discourse. These goals, or policy proposals, will be evaluated by their ability to authentically honor the icon of the Black Holy Family. In truth, none of the proposals or reforms will create a child welfare system in which anti-Black racism is eliminated. But I hope some of these proposed reforms, if achieved, will help in "'getting the ground ready' for broader shifts in economy and culture."[14]

PROPER SUPPORT FOR IMPOVERISHED FAMILIES AND ELIMINATION OF FINANCIAL INCENTIVES

In 1964, President Lyndon Johnson unveiled his legislation for the war on poverty. This included food stamps, Medicare

13 Day, *Religious Resistance to Neoliberalism*, 164.
14 Day, *Religious Resistance to Neoliberalism*, 167.

and Medicaid, job programs, and the diversion of significant federal funds to elementary and secondary education. In 1975, the passage of the Earned Income Tax Credit began providing money for low-income families and has become the third largest antipoverty program in the United States.[15] These programs have made a significant dent in poverty rates, though much has been done since to defund antipoverty programs.

When welfare began in 1935, it was seen as directly tied to benefiting child welfare. The same was true of other antipoverty programs that followed. But by the late twentieth century, financial assistance for families—whether in the form of welfare or other antipoverty programs—was no longer viewed as part of the services provided for child welfare. Particularly on the local level, antipoverty programs and CPS services are separate and distinct. The CPS system operates under the assumption that economic opportunities in the United States are available to all. (This is also an assumption held by most Americans.) Therefore, it is believed that if a child is not being properly provided for, the fault is with the parents, not society.[16]

Previously, we discussed the obligation of federal agencies and federally funded programs to make reasonable accommodations to ensure services are not denied to someone because of a disability. In practice, this means CPS agencies have an obligation to work with disabled parents to ensure whether TPR is the only way to protect the child of a disabled parent from harm. Unfortunately, this obligation for disabled parents is often ignored by CPS agencies,

15 Emily Goff, Alison Acosta Fraser, and Romina Boccia, "Federal Spending by the Numbers 2013," *Heritage Foundation*, August 20, 2013, 11, https://www.heritage.org/budget-and-spending/report/federal-spending-the-numbers-2013-government-spending-trends-graphics (accessed July 25, 2021).

16 Lindsey, *Welfare of Children*, 23.

and the parents do not possess the resources to combat this systemic problem. Hopefully, a class action suit in the near future will force CPS agencies to cease their negligence in this area.

I would like to take this obligation one step further. Though it is not currently the law, US families would greatly benefit if CPS were obligated *in every instance* to do everything possible to preserve families before taking steps to terminate parental rights. Just as CPS investigators and caseworkers often assume that a mother with a cognitive delay cannot care for her children, CPS workers often judge too quickly that impoverished Black mothers cannot properly care for their children. A mandate requiring CPS to exhaust every other option before deciding to terminate parental rights would require a shift in resources. Such a change would shift CPS from an individualist perspective that views every person as having equitable access to resources to a communal-responsibility perspective that realizes not all people have equal opportunities. Such a perspective would work to ensure everyone has the available resources to properly care for their family. This is the perspective of CST, and it acknowledges the world is unjust and that concrete steps are necessary to rectify injustice and protect families. This perspective would work to ensure families are never separated because of anti-Black racism or poverty. Currently, it is common to hear CPS workers complain they can only offer limited resources and that their work would benefit from certain antipoverty programs.

Dorothy Roberts suggests the racist child welfare system must be addressed on three fronts. First, proper financial supports are needed (e.g., an increased minimum wage, a guaranteed income, affordable housing, and universal healthcare). As the majority of child maltreatment is linked to neglect caused by poverty, this would address the primary needs of most families visited by CPS. Second is the creation of Black institutions to which CPS agencies would be held responsible. Third is to move away from a punitive CPS system to one that supports the preservation of families.[17] To claims that such programs are too costly and give the government too much power, Roberts counters that these problems already exist in the current child welfare system and are being ignored.[18]

Since the most common reason families come into contact with CPS is poverty, funding for improved antipoverty programs could come from the current CPS budget. Many states are currently able to redirect welfare funds to CPS, but this situation should ideally be reversed to aid impoverished families. Even if there is not the political will to do this, the CPS budget should still be cut because of the harm it is currently doing to impoverished and Black families. If we could prevent the needless separation of families, there would be compounded savings for the federal government. Fewer family separations and adoptions would eliminate many of the payments made to foster parents and adoptive parents, some of whom earn two thousand dollars per month for fostering or adopting a child. We could eliminate the salaries of many CPS workers, lawyers, judges, and outsourced contracts.

When the issue of money is brought up, I often think about Monique, whose children were taken away at a cost to the taxpayer of over $10,500 per month. For the eighteen months that a private agency was working on her case in Milwaukee, taxpayers were billed nearly $190,000. A housing voucher for $2,000 or less could have solved Monique's financial crisis and saved taxpayers about $188,000. The amount of money wasted on the CPS system is tremendous. But the current cultural mentality in the United States would rather refuse $2,000 to a Black mother and spend $190,000 on white middle-class professionals to punish that family for being Black and living in poverty.

17 Roberts, *Shattered Bonds*, 268–76.

18 Roberts, *Shattered Bonds*, 269.

Amada Morales believes a key component to the solution will involve "cutting the financial incentives to the middle-class bourgeoisie professionals who profit from the job creation of the CPS apparatus."[19] This statement echoes the sentiment of James Baldwin, who stated:

> Anyone, for example, who has worked in, or witnessed, any of the "anti-poverty" programs in the American ghetto has an instant understanding of "foreign aid" in the "under-developed" nations. In both locales, the most skillful adventurers improve their material lot; the most dedicated of the natives are driven mad or inactive—or underground—by frustration; while the misery of the hapless, voiceless millions is increased—and not only that; their reaction to their misery is described to the world as criminal. Nowhere is this grisly pattern clearer than it is in America today.[20]

The Bureau of Milwaukee Child Welfare built a brand-new office building in 2013 at a cost of ten million dollars.[21] This was money that could have been used to aid families struggling financially—who are forced to make decisions between paying for rent, food, or heat. Instead, these funds were utilized so that "middle-class bourgeoisie professionals" would have a respectable building in which to make decisions that will forever affect the lives of impoverished and African American families in the County of Milwaukee.

It is commonplace for political conservatives to express concerns that those living in poverty in the United States

19 Morales, interview, March 26, 2020.

20 James Baldwin, "No Name in the Street," in *James Baldwin: Collected Essays*, ed. Toni Morrison (New York: Library of America, 1998), 405.

21 Dave Reid, "A New Look for 27th Street," *Urban Milwaukee*, July 19, 2013, https://urbanmilwaukee.com/2013/07/19/friday-photos-a-new-look-for-27th-street/ (accessed August 5, 2020).

are becoming dependent on social programs. This concern is voiced despite the fact that there are not enough living-wage jobs for all Americans. What is less common is the concern that many middle-class families are becoming financially dependent on jobs that exploit the poverty of low-wage households and a racist culture that further impoverishes Black families through its mechanisms of distrust and control. To be sure, there are countless hardworking individuals who make up the staff of these social programs and are doing everything within their power to address the needs of America's impoverished, but the line between helping those in poverty and benefiting financially from them can often be blurry. Resources need to be directed to eliminating destitution, not just giving folks enough to barely get by. Where that is not possible, jobs that benefit financially from an impoverished class of people should be primarily awarded to Black and lower-class families.

Amada Morales also disapproves of state adoption assistance programs, which provide monthly subsidies to many families that adopt foster care children. Rates vary from state to state but generally increase where there is a perceived difficulty in having a child adopted. In Wisconsin, where Morales advocates, being a child of color can qualify adoptive parents for these subsidies, up to two thousand dollars per month depending on the exact circumstances. This is in addition to Medicaid coverage for the child and other eligible reimbursements until the child turns eighteen. Morales finds it "disgraceful" that white adoptive parents from the suburbs can receive more money each month for adopting a child than a Black single mother on welfare who is struggling to provide for her children.[22]

22 Morales, interview, March 26, 2020. Information on the adoption assistance subsidy can be found at https://www.nacac.org/help/adoption-assistance/adoption-assistance-us/.

THE ABOLITION OF CPS

The notion of liberation often includes the destruction of oppressive systems. With regard to the injustices present in policing and the prison industrial complex, there are regular cries of "Abolish prisons!" and "Abolish the police!" One of the proposals often associated with abolishing or defunding the police is an alternative response in which social workers would be sent to address certain 911 calls. Although sending social workers instead of police for some situations sounds benign, it has been the sending out of social workers that has led to over 170,000 children being removed from the custody of their parents on a yearly basis. Social workers, with the backing of county courts, can cause irreparable harm to families.

Carlos Morales, a former CPS investigator, argues that when all the harm caused by CPS is taken into account, "the world would be better off without CPS."[23] With the hundreds of thousands of families affected by CPS on an annual basis and the harm it has caused to the Black family in recent decades, the question must be asked: Should we abolish CPS? Based on advocacy work to reform CPS over the last twenty-plus years with no real progress, Dorothy Roberts advocates abolition, stating, "The family policing system can't be fixed."[24] Roberts believes abolition is the best way to "support families and keep children safe."[25]

If CPS were abolished from US society but nothing else changed, child welfare would be primarily addressed from a criminal justice perspective. This would greatly reduce the number of families that could be scrutinized and result in cases only being investigated for abuse or gross neglect. The

23 Carlos Morales, *Legally Kidnapped: The Case against Child Protective Services*, 2nd ed. (Lexington, KY: CreateSpace Independent Publishing Platform, 2015), 17. There is no relation between Amada Morales and Carlos Morales.

24 Roberts, *Torn Apart*, 9–10, 27.

25 Roberts, *Torn Apart*, 284.

primary benefit to families would be the allocation of greater rights afforded to those charged with a crime and raising the standard for conviction to "beyond a reasonable doubt" rather than the "preponderance of evidence" required in family court. Therefore, solid evidence would be required to separate families, who could no longer be separated based on second- and third-hand hearsay.

In another sense, CPS abolition is not a new concept or practice. As Roberts observes, "This nation has already created communities where the child welfare system has been abolished, but it has reserved them for elite white families." Roberts believes this is evidence that if all families had their basic needs met, CPS would "cease to be necessary."[26]

Another potential benefit of this option would be greater transparency. It is difficult to hold the child welfare system accountable when everything is considered confidential. Greater public scrutiny of cases would lead to fewer children being removed. Unfortunately, the anti-Black culture present in the criminal justice system would result in more Black parents being charged with crimes against their children than their white counterparts. The public record of these allegations—even if false—could result in parents having increased difficulty in finding work and housing. Nevertheless, a parent would rather have an unfounded charge of abuse on their public record than have their parental rights terminated.

A likely negative impact of this proposal is the case where some families may be separated by having a parent put in prison, which previously may have been handled through a CPS home plan or TPR. Black parents would likely be sent to prison more often than white parents in similar situations. Furthermore, a criminal court would require children, who were able, to testify, which many believe would revictimize the child.[27]

26 Roberts, *Torn Apart*, 292.

27 Shapiro and Maras, *Multidisciplinary Investigation*, 297, 330.

It must also be admitted that there are different goals for CPS workers and law enforcement. The primary concern of CPS workers is supposed to be making sure the child is safe and creating a safety plan if one is warranted. They are tasked with looking out for the best interests of the child. The primary concern of law enforcement is supposed to be discovering if a crime occurred and, if so, apprehending the perpetrator.[28] Although criminal courts could be adapted to work more toward family preservation rather than punitive imprisonment for lower classes of crimes, this would require a major restructuring of the system, which could essentially recreate CPS.

To some extent, criminal courts are already involved and complement CPS. Criminal courts regularly hear the worst cases of physical abuse and neglect that resulted in death, long-term trauma, or permanent injuries, as well as sexual abuse.[29] Depending on what action is being taken by CPS, prosecutors may not pursue a case or may decide to have both the family court and criminal court cases proceed simultaneously. The prosecutor has broad discretion and determines this on a case-by-case basis.[30] As long as anti-Black racism is a cultural problem in the United States, shifting child welfare completely over to the criminal justice system is unappealing, though it may be a better short-term solution than allowing CPS to continue with little to no oversight.

The best-case scenario would likely be the dismantling of CPS while installing dignified mechanisms to support impoverished families. As previously mentioned, universal basic income is probably the best support the federal government could institute. With the funds saved from no longer funding CPS and other antipoverty programs that

28 Shapiro and Maras, *Multidisciplinary Investigation*, 297.
29 Shapiro and Maras, *Multidisciplinary Investigation*, 327.
30 Shapiro and Maras, *Multidisciplinary Investigation*, 327.

require massive overhead, a universal basic income program could be instituted without raising taxes. Before his murder, Dr. Martin Luther King Jr. was planning a Poor People's Campaign that would involve massive nonviolent direct action in Washington, DC. One of his goals with that campaign was establishing a universal basic income, which he believed would instill dignity and self-determination into those impoverished as well as reduce "personal conflicts" within the family.[31] If King had lived and his campaign had been successful, CPS might have remained a mostly voluntary program for parents seeking help in raising their children.

In her discussion of CPS abolition, Roberts introduces the notion of "nonreformist reforms." This is a strategy employed in prison and police abolition circles. According to this approach, one should only support reforms that work toward weakening, slowing down, dismantling, and defunding CPS. With this in mind, Roberts suggests the following proposals: (1) requiring CPS workers to provide parents with a list of their rights, (2) putting a ban on involuntary drug tests, (3) eliminating the fifteen-month rule, (4) having a lawyer assigned to a family before a CPS investigation, (5) diverting financial resources from CPS to families in poverty and reparations for families that were forcibly separated, (6) helping separated families reunite, and (7) making foster care voluntary.[32]

OTHER PROPOSALS

The first part of this chapter offered three main proposals in addressing child welfare: (1) a different narrative in which

31 Martin Luther King Jr., "Where Do We Go from Here," in *The Radical King*, ed. Cornel West (Boston: Beacon Press, 2015), 172–73.

32 Roberts, *Torn Apart*, 295–99.

the dignity and worth of Black families are recognized, (2) a redirection of financial resources from systems that separate impoverished and Black families to systems that promote and protect these families, and (3) CPS abolition. The remainder of this chapter will assess other proposals that are often offered as potential ways to fix the current CPS system.

A Collaborative Approach

There is a CPS model that attempts to be less adversarial and more collaborative. It is called *differential response*, but it is also at times referred to as *alternate response*, *family assessment response*, or *multiple-track response*. It is favored by many Democrats because it is perceived as shifting the focus from an adversarial experience where people might lose their children to a collaborative one to preserve families. This method often involves contracting community organizations with certain specialties to interact with families. It hopes to keep children with their parents while providing critical services to strengthen parenting and the family dynamic. Some states, such as Missouri and Minnesota, began implementing differential response programs in the early 1990s for families where they believed the children could remain safely in the home.[33]

Although this brief summary of the differential response makes it sound more positive than the traditional CPS response, this approach promotes greater government intrusion. It often leads to more families coming into contact with CPS than would happen otherwise since this method promotes regular interaction between service providers and impoverished and Black families. Increased interaction with CPS can have the unintended effect of eventually leading to the removal of one's children and TPR. It has the benefit of

33 Ronald C. Hughes et al., "Issues in Differential Response," *Research on Social Worker Practice* 23, no. 5 (September 2013): 493–530, on pp. 493–94.

increasing resources to families but statistically only has a negligible effect on preventing removals.[34]

Even for families where child neglect could not be substantiated, these services may be strongly suggested by caseworkers. Research suggests that one of the dangers of differential response is that it is resource intensive and focuses limited resources on low-risk children and families that do not warrant intervention. This leaves fewer resources to support children and families with more difficult and complex situations that could be preserved if adequate resources were available.[35] Furthermore, as with the traditional CPS process, there is no way to truly ascertain the effectiveness of differential response.[36]

Training as Part of the Solution

Cultural competency and implicit bias training are sorely needed at all levels of the CPS system, from investigators and caseworkers to lawyers and judges. Anti-racism training needs to be a prerequisite for improving CPS interactions in the short term. Significant long-term changes will only occur when we become a society that values the Black family. Short-term achievements should not be viewed as final victories, and they should never be the sole focus of one's resources.

Nevertheless, workers need to learn about the effects of structural racism in US culture and racial bias in CPS. CPS needs to dive deeper into its own racial-disparity data and employ this data to compare how each county and state compared to others in regard to racial disparity. This data can also be utilized to reveal which CPS investigators, case

34 Dale, "Addressing the Underlying Issue of Poverty." This footnote is in reference to the negligible effect.

35 Hughes et al., "Issues in Differential Response," 504.

36 Ellett, "Timely and Needed Perspectives on Differential Response in Child Protective Services," 522, 524.

managers, lawyers, and judges exhibit patterns of explicit or implicit racial bias. Those who are found to exhibit these patterns will need to correct those problems or be removed.

Let's take the healthcare field as an example. As previously mentioned, Black children suffer greater rates of low birth weights even when income, prenatal care, and education are taken into account. Obviously, health professionals cannot control the racism experienced by patients outside the healthcare system. Regardless, a recent *Child Trends* article offers the following as recommendations to combat low birth weights for Black children in healthcare settings: (1) educate medical professionals and staff on implicit bias and cultural competency (*cultural competency* refers to the ability of healthcare professionals to understand, communicate with, and effectively interact with patients with diverse values, beliefs, and feelings); (2) provide Black mothers with clinical and social support, such as doulas, whose involvement with a birthing mother lowers the likelihood of birth complications by almost half; and (3) have hospitals break down their own data on birth complications by race to be more aware of their failures and areas for growth. Such data may also help identity medical staff who are particularly prone to implicit racial bias.[37]

Training for CPS workers should also include emphasizing the proper attitude to have toward parents. Research illustrates that the attitude and actions of CPS social workers toward parents affect the outcome. Workers are better received by parents if they are perceived to be caring, genuine, empathetic, and nonjudgmental. Active listening and

37 Alexandria Wilkins, Victoria Efetevbia, and Esther Gross, "Reducing Implicit Bias, Raising Quality of Care May Reduce High Maternal Mortality Rates for Black Women," *Child Trends*, April 25, 2019, https://www.childtrends.org/reducing-implicit-bias-raising-quality-care-may-reduce-high-maternal-mortality-rates-black-women (accessed July 29, 2020).

providing extra help can also improve the perception of workers by parents. These attitudes and actions build relationships with parents that make the workers' legitimate critiques and feedback more palatable and increase the chances of positive changes in parental behaviors and reunification. Workers who are perceived as judgmental, cold and uncaring, refusing to listen, overly critical, and insincere are more likely to face hostility from parents.[38]

In addition, a discerning CPS worker can make the difference between a legitimate removal and unjust family separation. The North Carolina social services attorney and former foster care social worker Angenette Stephenson advises CPS workers to "differentiate between the parent who cannot safely parent his or her child and the parent who is emotionally volatile and blames everyone else for his or her circumstances. Often, they can be the same person, but sometimes they are not. Sometimes the difficult parent with the vendetta against the social worker can actually parent fairly well."[39] This can be especially true for parents who had negative experiences with CPS when they were children. Stephenson's advice resonates with my experience in Milwaukee. The social workers who we regularly see in court advocating for TPR for good parents are often reacting to the vitriolic attitude of the parent toward the worker without recognizing real parenting ability.

Smaller caseloads could also benefit CPS workers and families. Often, CPS agencies overburden caseworkers, who already have a high burnout rate. The exact number of cases permitted a worker needs to be fluid, taking into account the number of children in each case and the specific issues facing

38 Sarah Maiter, Sally Palmer, and Shehenaz Manji, "Strengthening Social Worker-Client Relationship in Child Protective Services," in *Child Maltreatment*, ed. John E. B. Myers (Los Angeles: Sage, 2012), 18–33.

39 Angenette Stephenson, quoted in Pollack, "Attorney Perspectives of Child Protective Services 'Legal Kidnapping,'" 24, 36, on p. 24.

a family.[40] In creating a more specific determination, caseworkers and managers should collaborate to determine what constitutes a manageable caseload. Hopefully, this will not be used as an excuse to hire more caseworkers but rather to limit the number of families under CPS scrutiny and focus on the cases where children are actually suffering harm or are in real danger.

Other Basic Reforms

This section will assess several other possible reforms that do not each warrant an entire section. These include video recording interviews with potential child victims, providing parent advocates, presenting parents with a copy of their rights during their first interaction with CPS, relaxing the time limit to terminate parental rights simply because a child has been in out-of-home care for fifteen of the last twenty-two months, and having the courts provide parents with a well-defined pathway to reunification.

One short-term solution and positive development would be video-recording interviews with potential child victims and making the recordings available to the parents and their lawyers.[41] Children—especially young children—are very susceptible to leading questions, but one cannot tell from a CPS investigator's report if a child was unbiasedly questioned. In fact, it is well documented that asking a young child about an event that did not occur can result in a false memory of that event. Even reporting an event to young children can result in a child having a detailed false memory of an event they did not witness.[42] Just as the recording of police officers has uncovered grave injustices that would have otherwise gone unnoticed, the recording of

40 Shapiro and Maras, *Multidisciplinary Investigation*, 379.

41 Krason, "Mondale Act," 60.

42 Angela D. Moore, "False Memories and Young Child Witnesses," *New Criminal Law Review* 19, no. 1 (winter 2016): 125–39, on p. 127.

child interviews with CPS investigators would allow parents and their lawyers to see if any leading questions or narratives were directed at the children.

Parental advocates, which were mentioned earlier in the chapter, could also play a role in preserving families. Parents need resources from outside the CPS system that can be there to guide them through the process when they are at a financial disadvantage and cannot afford to hire a good lawyer. Amada Morales is the perfect example of an outsider who guides parents through this process. She is the equivalent of a doula for parents trying to navigate the CPS system to have their children returned with as few complications as possible.

David Tobis authored a 2013 book documenting how parents pressured New York State to have CPS agencies hire parent advocates—specifically people who had previously had their children removed. As Tobis states, "The advocates were parents who had overcome ordinary and extraordinary difficulties—fighting uncontrollably with their adolescent children, depression, drug and alcohol addiction, living on the street, and domestic violence. These parents had changed their lives, [and] reunited with their children." Now the advocates work with parents on navigating CPS to reunite with their children. Originally, these advocates were seen as enemies by CPS. Now they are viewed as partners who create better outcomes for New York's CPS.[43] Although parent advocates have resulted in a tremendous decrease in foster care, there are still neither enough parent advocates to meet the need nor enough funds to hire the required number.[44]

Amada Morales urges courts and judges to allow parents to bring an advocate or friend to court proceedings. Because of the secrecy and privacy concerns surrounding child-maltreatment cases, impoverished parents usually have to face the courtroom alone or only with a court-appointed

43 Tobis, *From Pariahs to Partners*, x.
44 Tobis, *From Pariahs to Partners*, xi.

lawyer. As previously noted, court-appointed lawyers are often unhelpful and provide advice that is detrimental to the parent's case. Since the majority of CPS jurisdictions do not provide parent advocates, parents should be permitted to bring their own support person to court hearings to combat feelings of isolation and to offer support and advice. These support people may also remember critical details from court hearings that parents may forget in the midst of an emotional hearing. Furthermore, parents with a low IQ or learning disability can have a particularly difficult time understanding what is happening in court.[45]

Also in the short term, parents need to know their rights. Since parents often do not have advance notice of a CPS investigator stopping by their home, it would be most helpful for the investigator to provide parents with a copy of their rights before they are permitted to make any requests. An example of something that could be handed out can be found in Appendix: Quick CPS Guide for Parents. Although not included in the appendix, if parents are found innocent of any maltreatment, they should demand that their names and the names of their children be expunged from any CPS databases. If one's data stays in the system, one is more likely to be confronted by CPS again. As the conservative political scientist Joe Wolverton warns, "If your name remains in the CPS database, then caseworkers are able to monitor your family, and your 'records' are sent to a number of individuals with whom your children might have contact—doctors, teachers, or therapists, for example—and they are all alerted that you are being 'watched' by CPS, and are required to report anything they deem to be of concern."[46] Since these professionals are already mandated reporters, this is unnecessary and could lead to snap judgments as well as traumatic and inappropriate CPS intervention in the family's

45 Amada Morales, interview by author, Milwaukee, WI, January 6, 2020.
46 Wolverton, "Help!," 23.

life. Additionally, if a parent plans to work with children in the future, being in a CPS database may affect their ability to obtain employment. The database used in Wisconsin is the Caregiver Misconduct Registry and Rehab Review. For the Wisconsin database, a parent's name is only supposed to be on this list if there is a substantiated finding of child maltreatment.[47]

A short-term change that should be made on the federal level is to delay the petition to terminate parental rights simply because a child has been in out-of-home care for fifteen of the last twenty-two months. Although children spend far too much time out of the home, this ticking clock leads to the permanent separation of families without legitimate cause. The clock may run out for some parents because CPS workers are not providing the necessary resources that are required by the court in a timely manner. If the parent is disgruntled about this, they may have to wait months to tell the judge when they finally get back to court.

Even specialists in the field have misconceptions about this fifteen-month clock. Lauren Shapiro and Marie-Helen Maras advocate that the only exception to the fifteen-month rule should be medical emergencies. They complain, "Parents often decide (or at the very least inform the family court) at the last minute that they want to comply with the requirements imposed on them."[48] As they explain it, "Parental rights are terminated within 15–23 months of the failure of a parent to comply with the family court requirements or the case plan provided by CPS."[49] I wish it were true that parents would normally have their children returned after complying with the court's requirements or a case plan, but parents regularly have their rights terminated even after a CPS worker confirms on the stand that the parent has fulfilled the court's

47 Morales, interview, January 6, 2020.

48 Shapiro and Maras, *Multidisciplinary Investigation*, 377.

49 Shapiro and Maras, *Multidisciplinary Investigation*, 377.

requirements. The justification is that the worker still believes the parent is not fit to care for their child. For example, they may believe the mother is too angry or behaves inappropriately. There are often vague "feelings" that lead a CPS worker to their determinations, to which judges will often add their perfunctory assent in their final decisions.

In responding to the situation of a single father who had completed his court-mandated courses in an attempt to have his daughter returned, Milwaukee County Circuit Court Judge Christopher Foley commented that there is no Wisconsin law mandating the return of a child simply because a parent complied with a court-ordered program. He continued, "The judge has to make a determination on what's in the best interest of the child," he continued.[50] I include this statement from Judge Foley not to comment on the specific case in question but to emphasize that once a child is placed in foster care, the doctrine of the best interests of the child can override any corrective action taken by the parent if the judge feels the child's situation would be improved by growing up in another household. Even when parents go over and above what was requested by the court, they may never be reunited with their child simply because the court deems a suburban foster family to have more financial resources with which to care for a child.

CONCLUSION

This chapter offered long- and short-term proposals to ameliorate the harm caused by CPS in an anti-Black culture and to promote authentic freedom for the Black family. None of these proposals is a cure-all. Some of them—as noted—could even do more harm than good. And we should be

50 Christopher Foley, quoted in Eric Ross, "Fighting with Child Welfare System," WTMJ-TV Milwaukee, April 29, 2016, https://www.tmj4.com/news/i-team/father-says-fighting-with-child-welfare-system-is-a-losing-battle (accessed December 17, 2019).

wary of expending significant resources on short-term goals at the expense of the long-term vision. In the end, as long as white supremacy is a defining characteristic of US culture, CPS as a manifestation of US anti-Blackness must be recognized. Therefore, any proposed solution needs to be careful not to conflate poverty and racism. Though interrelated, efforts that only address poverty will fail to confront racism. The acknowledgment that there are good CPS workers and foster parents does not rectify a racist system.

This book has brought forth resources from CST, Scripture, and Black scholars that can aid churches and society to cultivate the theological implications for a society that subjugates Black families in the name of the best interests of the child. Since anti-Blackness is woven into our cultural fabric, we need to recognize there will be no quick fixes. In Latina feminist and *mujerista* theologies, there is the notion of *un poquito de justicia*, which literally means "a little bit of justice." This version of liberation theology recognizes that the complete eradication of unjust systems is unrealistic in the short term, but "just a little bit of justice continues the momentum in the cry and struggle for life."[51]

As noted in chapter 1, we saw a shift in child welfare focus during the twentieth century. The century began with a belief in the tender-years doctrine, which proposed it was best for young children to be with their mother. With the Social Security Act of 1935, the federal government began providing welfare payments to mothers—primarily white—to ensure that they would not lose their children due to poverty. At this point, foster care was a largely voluntary program available to mostly white families.

The successes of the civil rights movement of the late 1950s and 1960s led to greater access to welfare and other

51 Neomi De Anda, "Latina Feminist and *Mujerista* Theologies as Political Theologies," in *T&T Clark Handbook of Political Theology*, ed. Rubén Rosario Rodríguez (London: T&T Clark, 2020), 271–83, on p. 274.

antipoverty programs for African Americans. In the wake of this diversification in who could receive welfare and other antipoverty program funds, we saw the creation of the modern CPS system, where foster care was no longer used as a voluntary option but employed as a weapon to attack Black families. It was during this time that the philosophy of the child welfare system shifted from the tender-years doctrine to the best interests of the child, which has always been used as an excuse for removing children and terminating parental rights. Through a combination of intentional and unintentional acts of anti-Black racism, the best interests of the child doctrine grew out of a racist foundation, and it has never stopped being used to attack the Black family.

I will close with one of the more difficult passages found in the Gospels: Jesus's cursing of the fig tree (Mark 11:12–21, NABRE). Jesus is on his way to the Temple and sees a fig tree. He finds no figs on the tree and shouts out, "May no one ever eat of your fruit again!" Jesus shouts this curse even though we are told by the narrator that it was not the time of year when figs were found. Jesus then goes to the Temple, is disgusted by the presence of the money changers, and drives them out. The next day, Jesus and his disciples pass the same fig tree on their way to the Temple. Peter remarks to the group that the tree is now withered all the way to its roots.

On the face of it, this story seems unfair. Why did Jesus ruin a perfectly good tree when it was not even time for its fruit to be in season? Whether this story is based on actual events is unknown. We do know that the Gospel of Mark contained many story sandwiches, meaning the author liked to split up a story and put a related story in the middle. Mark sandwiches the cleansing of the Temple in the middle of the fig tree story. It was another way for the author to state he did not believe the Temple was bearing fruit. In this way, the withering of the fig tree foreshadowed the destruction of the Temple by the Roman Empire in 70 CE.

I share this story not to explore the relationship of the fig tree and the Temple but rather to talk about the oppressive CPS system and the best interests of the child doctrine, which has attacked the freedom of the Black family in the United States for decades. It is like a fig tree that is not in season. Ideally, it would be bearing fruit—meaning it would protect children from abuse and provide resources for struggling families so they may determine their own futures. Unfortunately, that is not the case. The question at this point is whether the tree can be saved with proper fertilizing and care or if it is time to curse the tree and let it wither. One could argue that fruit is produced when some children are protected despite the alarming rate of impoverished and Black families that are needlessly separated and oppressed. But a few good pieces of fruit in the wake of devastation is not a good harvest. Moving forward, we must place ourselves in this parable. Having seen the fig tree, how shall we respond?

APPENDIX

Quick CPS Guide for Parents

Below is a quick guide for parents whose lives have been disrupted by CPS. Please read the entire guide before taking any action.

(1) NEVER MEET A CASEWORKER AT YOUR HOME ALONE.

Do not meet with caseworkers at your home or alone. Ask friends or relatives to be present for the meeting and develop questions to ask the worker. Have your support people write down notes. The most important question to ask is what the safety concerns are and how to cure them. It is wise to let CPS into your home as long as you are not alone, it is not a surprise visit, and they did not bring the police. If police are present, only let them in if they have a warrant.

(2) ASK FOR THE SPECIFIC ALLEGATIONS.

Ask the caseworker what the allegations are before they meet with you. If your children are removed, ask the caseworker to specify the safety concerns that are preventing your children from being home. Find a solution to eliminate these concerns. Do not settle for vague answers such as *abuse* or *neglect*. Those are categories, not details. You are entitled to know which specific acts you are accused of committing. You must focus on solving the safety concerns to close your CPS case.

(3) LIMIT YOUR CONVERSATION.

Limit your conversation with the caseworkers. You want to explain your situation to the caseworker, but they are there to find evidence to support what they already believe to be true—that you abused or neglected your child.

(4) RECORD EVERYTHING.

Record your interactions with CPS workers as much as possible. If the workers know they're being recorded, it will make them less likely to prolong the meeting. If a CPS worker wants to interview your child, tell them you would like a support person present and you want it recorded. Provide your own recorder in case the worker's recorder malfunctions.

(5) HAVE A TRUSTED DOCTOR EXAMINE YOUR CHILD.

Make your trusted pediatrician and therapist aware of the CPS involvement. These professionals are authorized to tell the judge if your children should be with you. Speak to them about strategies you are using to cure any suspected safety concerns. If your children are removed, these two witnesses will hold the most credibility for the judge. If you do not already have a family therapist for you and your children, find one fast. Find one who can relate to you and whom you can trust. Do not go to a doctor recommended by CPS. Find your own medical professionals.

(6) FIND FAMILY AND FRIENDS WHO ARE WILLING TO TAKE YOUR CHILDREN.

Collect the names of friends and relatives who are willing and able to care for your children in case CPS decides to take them. CPS is required by law to place them with family or friends before considering strangers but will often ignore this law. If your children must spend time away from you, it is better that it be with people you know and trust than potentially antagonistic foster parents. It is also more difficult for CPS to terminate your parental rights when children are placed with relatives.

(7) READ THE COMPLAINTS FILED AGAINST YOU AND REMOVE ANY FALSE ALLEGATIONS FROM THE PETITION.

Parents are routinely accused of ridiculous things. Be sure you are aware of the allegations and safety concerns in the complaint. At the first hearing, parents often stipulate (or agree) unknowingly to the accusations in the petition without realizing they agreed with false allegations. These allegations will become key pieces of a case to terminate parental rights months or years after the initial court hearing. Have your lawyer advocate to remove any false allegation from the petition. The allegations to which you stipulate will be held against you for the duration of the case.

(8) STAY CALM.

Caseworkers can be very frustrating and unprofessional. Keep your composure and use your energy to address safety concerns and court-ordered conditions. Caseworkers can use your anger against you and say that you are abusive, have mental deficiencies, or have not made a behavioral change. Find a third party, such as your lawyer or a community advocate, to bring any complaints against a caseworker to the judge or the worker's supervisor.

(9) HELP YOUR LAWYER WIN THE CASE.

If you cannot afford a lawyer who specializes in CPS cases, be sure to help your court-appointed lawyer win your case.

Meet with your lawyer to prepare for upcoming court hearings and find ways to address the allegations against you. Be polite—but assertive—with your lawyer. Once you have met all of your court-ordered conditions, you must convince your lawyer to file a change of placement back to you. If you are contesting the allegations against you in a jury trial, ask your lawyer to go over the legal strategy with you. Make a witness list for your lawyer and go over it.

(10) BE AWARE OF THE TIME LIMIT.

By law, the courts will begin termination of parental rights proceedings once a child has been in out-of-home care for fifteen of the last twenty-two months. Meet your conditions and correct safety concerns as soon as possible. Do not wait for any party to file a motion to return your children. Press your lawyer to file a change of placement as soon as you meet your conditions. After this filing, it will normally take months for the judge to make a ruling.

Index of Subjects and Names